Presented to:

_____

From:

_____

JESUS CALLING®

365 DEVOTIONS
FOR KIDS

SARAH YOUNG

Adapted by Tama Fortner

Edited by Kris Bearss

An Imprint of Thomas Nelson

Tommy Nelson, PO Box 141000, Nashville, TN 37214

Published in Nashville, Tennessee, by Tommy Nelson. Tommy Nelson is an imprint of Thomas Nelson. Thomas Nelson is a registered trademark of HarperCollins Christian Publishing, Inc.

Unless otherwise noted, Scripture quotations used in this book are from: The Holy Bible, New International Version®. © 1973, 1978, 1984 by Biblica. Used by permission of Zondervan. All rights reserved.

Scripture quotations marked cev are taken from the Contemporary English Version, © 1991, 1992, 1995 American Bible Society. Used by permission.

Scripture quotations marked icb are taken from The Holy Bible, International Children's Bible © 1986, 1988, 1999 by Thomas Nelson. Used by permission. All rights reserved.

Scripture quotations marked kjv are taken from the King James Version of the Bible. Public domain.

Scripture quotations marked nasb are taken from the New American Standard Bible®. Copyright © 1960, 1962, 1963, 1968, 1971, 1972, 1973, 1975, 1977, 1995 by The Lockman Foundation. Used by permission. www.Lockman.org

Scripture quotations marked nkjv are taken from the New King James Version. © 1982 by Thomas Nelson. Used by permission. All rights reserved.

Scripture quotations marked nlt are taken from the Holy Bible, New Living Translation, copyright 1996, 2004 by Tyndale House Foundation. Used by permission of Tyndale House Ministries, Carol Stream, Illinois 60188. All rights reserved.

Cover design by Kathy Mitchell Design
Interior design by Mallory Collins

ISBN 978-1-4002-2498-2 (audiobook)
ISBN 978-1-4002-3749-4 (eBook)
ISBN 978-1-4002-1862-2 (HC)

Library of Congress Cataloging-in-Publication Data

Fortner, Tama, 1969–
    Jesus calling : 365 devotions for kids / Sarah Young ; adapted by Tama Fortner ; edited by Kris Bearss.
        p. cm.
    ISBN 978-1-4003-1634-2 (hardcover)
      1. Devotional calendars—Juvenile literature. I. Young, Sarah, 1946– II. Bearss, Kris. III. Young, Sarah, 1946– Jesus calling. IV. Title.
    BV4870.F67 2010
    242'.62—dc22
                                   2010017099

Printed in India

24 25 26 27 28 29 REP 10 9 8 7 6

I dedicate *Jesus Calling* to my mother, whose encouragement helped me keep working till I completed the book. She showed her appreciation of my writing in many ways. She kept my manuscript beside her bed, so she could read it every morning. Once, while away from her home, she even asked me to send her the readings day by day. After she died from cancer, I found portions of my writings that she had hand-copied into a journal. This mother who had prayed me through thick and thin opened her heart fully to my devotional writing. She was a master storyteller, and she talked about writing children's books someday. Though that day never came, there is a sense in which—through me—she has written this book.

Thank you, Nani! Your legacy lives on.

Introduction

I'm delighted to have four grandchildren—Elie, John, Caleb, and Esther Grace. These children are precious to me, and I want them to grow up knowing and loving Jesus. I want this for you too.

You can get to know Jesus by praying and reading your Bible. It's important to understand how much Jesus loves you—and to enjoy Him as the Friend who is always with you.

The devotions in this book are written as if Jesus is speaking right to you. So "I," "Me," "My," and "Mine" are always about Jesus. I wrote the devotions this way to help you know that Jesus is with you all the time. He knows everything about you, and He loves you more than you can imagine!

Jesus loves you *so much* that He died on the cross to take the punishment for your sins. If you have never asked Him to be your Savior—forgiving all your sins—I hope you will do that very soon. It's the most important decision you will ever make! All the promises of the Bible are for *you* when Jesus is your Savior.

The Bible is the only perfect Word of God, and there is a Scripture verse written out for each devotion. If you want to learn even more, there are more Scripture references for you to read on your own.

I hope you will find a quiet place and read these devotions slowly each day. Remember, Jesus is Immanuel—God with us. So He is God with *you*. I pray that you will enjoy His Presence and His Peace as you spend this time with Him.

Sarah Young

JANUARY

You will seek Me and find Me when you search for Me with all your heart.

—Jeremiah 29:13 (NASB)

January 1

Get Ready for the Adventure!

*"For I know the plans I have for you," declares the L*ORD*, "plans to prosper you and not to harm you, plans to give you hope and a future."*
—Jeremiah 29:11

It's a new year, and I have a great adventure planned for you. Come to Me with a heart that is willing to be changed. Don't make the same mistakes you made last year. This year, try doing things *My* way.

I know that trying something new can be frightening. But I also know *you*, and I understand you completely. You can trust Me to wrap you up in My Love—a love that never ends.

Whether you are at home or at school, talking with your friends or doing homework, keep Me in your thoughts. Let Me guide you. I will take you on a journey that will change who you are and how you see the world and the people around you. Yes, I have great plans for you, and I will be with you every step of the way!

READ ON YOUR OWN

Romans 12:2

Choose Me

But the Lord answered her, "Martha, Martha, you are getting worried and upset about too many things. Only one thing is important. Mary has chosen the right thing, and it will never be taken away from her."
—Luke 10:41–42 (ICB)

You are so very busy. But I want you to stop for a minute. Put down the game, hang up the phone, turn off the computer. Spend some time with Me.

Even now your thoughts are racing ahead to today's plans and problems. But put those thoughts and worries aside. Just think about Me and how much I love you. I know exactly what is going to happen in your life today. Don't worry. I will give you everything you need to face your day.

Please don't skimp on our time together. The computer and the telephone and the homework will still be there when our time is through. Choose Me first—and the blessings I give you will not be taken away.

READ ON YOUR OWN

Psalm 105:4; Luke 10:39-42

January 3

I Am Bigger Than the World

I have told you these things, so that in me you may have peace.
In this world you will have trouble. But take heart!
I have overcome the world.
—John 16:33

Think about how wonderful it feels to dive into a cool pool of water on a hot summer's day. That is what My Peace is like. It will refresh you and strengthen you. And that peace can be yours at all times.

As you go through your day, you will face problems and troubles. But you *never* have to face them alone. I am *always* with you. I am the best Friend that you will ever have. I walk beside you, to give you comfort and strength. I also walk ahead of you, so that I am ready to help you face whatever is coming. And I am within you, giving you a secret ability to think and act without fear.

There will be problems and hard times, but don't let them get you down. I have already overcome all the problems of this world. In Me you can find Peace.

READ ON YOUR OWN

Psalm 31:19–20

A New Habit

The Lord takes care of his people like a shepherd. He gathers the people like lambs in his arms. He carries them close to him. He gently leads the mothers of the lambs.
—Isaiah 40:11 (ICB)

Everyone has habits—some are good and some are not so good. Starting today, I want you to learn a new habit. Try saying, "I trust You, Jesus," no matter what is happening around you. Choose to remember that I am in control of the universe, and that I love you with a love that is higher than any mountain and deeper than any ocean.

By saying, "I trust You, Jesus," you are saying that you *know* I am in control of all things and that nothing can defeat Me. It is then that fear loses its grip on you. So when you are facing tough times, trust Me to guide you through them and use them to grow your faith. Trusting Me is a habit you won't ever want to break.

READ ON YOUR OWN

Psalm 63:2; Isaiah 40:10; Psalm 139:7–10

Winning My Way

But we live by faith, not by what we see.
—2 Corinthians 5:7 (CEV)

W hat does it mean to *win*? Your friends—and maybe even some grown-ups—may say that winning means never messing up, never failing. It is being the best, better than anyone else, and being in total control. That is how this world sees winning.

But I have another definition. Winning—for all eternity—is about letting *Me* have total control. It is admitting that you need Me, and then trusting Me to lead you.

Don't just ask Me to bless what you have already decided to do. Ask Me what I want for you. I may fill your heart with a dream that seems impossibly far beyond your reach. And that dream will be bigger than anything you can do on your own. But remember, nothing is beyond *My* reach.

Yes, you will mess up sometimes, and you will make mistakes. But when you depend on Me, I will use your mistakes to grow your faith and to help you win—*My way!*

READ ON YOUR OWN

Psalm 34:17–18

Dare to Dream My Dream

*Now to him who is able to do immeasurably more than all we ask
or imagine, according to his power that is at work within us,
to him be glory in the church and in Christ Jesus throughout
all generations, for ever and ever! Amen.*
—Ephesians 3:20–21

Dream your biggest, most incredible dream—and then know that I am able to do far more than that, far more than you could ever ask or imagine. Allow Me to fill your mind with *My* dreams for you.

Don't be discouraged if your prayers are not answered right away. Time is a great teacher. It teaches you to be patient and to trust in My perfect plan—even when you don't know what is going to happen next.

When everything seems way too hard, that is when you can truly see My Power at work in your life. Don't let this world's craziness drag you into worry. Instead, choose to see all that I am doing around you. Remember, there is no limit to what I can do.

READ ON YOUR OWN

Romans 8:6; Isaiah 40:30–31; Revelation 5:13

January 7

I Love That!

Give thanks whatever happens.
That is what God wants for you in Christ Jesus.
—1 Thessalonians 5:18 (ICB)

It is not possible to thank Me too much. I love your praises. Sometimes your praise is an unplanned, in-the-moment, you-just-can't-help-yourself sort of thing. Perhaps you have just received one of My blessings or have been overwhelmed by the beauty of My creation, and you are just bursting to tell Me about it. I love that!

Other times, you stop to think about My blessings, about My Presence in your life. And you decide to thank Me. I love that kind of praise too.

When you are struggling with a problem, pray about it. Then go ahead and thank Me for the help you know I will give you. This kind of praise means you know I am in control—and I love that!

Fill up the spare moments of your life with praise, and you will find that your life is filled with Me.

READ ON YOUR OWN

Psalm 22:3; Psalm 146:1–2

Sometimes I Whisper

God is our refuge and strength, an ever-present help in trouble.
—Psalm 46:1

I am *always* with you. Even now, I am here with you. That soft whisper in your mind? That's from Me. That gentle tap on your heart? That's from Me too. I have all the Power in heaven and on earth. With My Might, I can control the very wind and the waves, but with you I am quiet and tender. And the more you are hurting, the more tender I am.

When others leave you feeling worthless and alone, hope in Me. My hope is not just a wish for things to be better; it is My promise to you that I will always help you. I will carry your troubles for you and lighten your heart. I am your ever-present Help, so you are never alone.

READ ON YOUR OWN

Romans 12:12; Romans 15:13

January 9

Never Give Up!

Nothing is impossible for God!
—Luke 1:37 (CEV)

I am always with you and for you. I am your biggest fan. When you decide to do something that fits My plans for you, nothing in heaven or on earth can stop you. You may face some problems along the way to your goal—that is part of living in an imperfect world. But never give up! With My help, you can conquer any problem.

But don't just rush headlong toward your goal, trying to make things happen when you want them to. First, come to Me. Ask Me to guide you every step of the way, minute by minute. Let Me set the pace. Sometimes I may ask you to wait, or to slow down, or even to stop for a while. But remember, My timing is perfect. Trust Me and enjoy sharing the journey with Me.

READ ON YOUR OWN

Romans 8:31; Psalm 46:1–3; Luke 1:37

A Treasure of Trust

But store up for yourselves treasures in heaven,
where moth and rust do not destroy, and where thieves do not break in
and steal. For where your treasure is, there your heart will be also.
—Matthew 6:20–21

Every time you choose to trust Me, it's like putting a coin into My treasury. Like a bank, I keep these coins of trust safe for you. Over time, these coins add up, creating a wealth of trust for you to use when you need it. The more you choose to trust Me and My teaching, instead of just following your friends, the more I will help you trust Me.

Trusting takes practice. Start on quiet days, when nothing much seems to be happening. You will see that I really am faithful. Then, when trouble comes, you will know how to trust Me—because you have practiced. You will have saved up a heavenly treasure of trust that will see you through whatever troubles come your way.

READ ON YOUR OWN

Psalm 56:3–4

Let Go

*Jesus has the power of God. His power has given us everything
we need to live and to serve God. We have these things because we
know him. Jesus called us by his glory and goodness.*
—2 Peter 1:3 (ICB)

I magine that your life is a video game. Now, let go of the controls and let Me have control instead. That is what trust looks like. It is letting go and remembering that I am God. This is My world: I made it and I control it. You show your love for Me by letting Me have control in your life.

When you pray, I want you to share everything with Me: your joys and heartaches, your struggles and triumphs, your worries and questions. I am your best Friend—pour out your heart to Me. And then thank Me for the answers that are already on the way. When you trust Me to be in control, you can let go of your worries and live closer to Me.

READ ON YOUR OWN

Psalm 46:10; Colossians 4:2; 2 Peter 1:4

Start with Me

Remain in me, and I will remain in you.
—John 15:4 (NLT)

S tart your day with Me. You may have some ideas about what will happen today, but I know *exactly* what will happen.

I know you want to see the whole map of your day, every twist and turn, every joy and pain. You think that will help you be prepared for whatever you have to face. But *My* way is better. Let Me be your Guide. No, I won't show you every detail of your day, but I will give you everything you need to handle it.

Start your day with Me, and then keep in touch. If you find your thoughts wandering where they shouldn't, just whisper My Name. I'll guide you back to the right road, because I am the best map you'll ever find!

READ ON YOUR OWN

Exodus 33:14; John 15:5–7

Expect Surprises!

This is the day the Lord has made; let us rejoice and be glad in it.
—Psalm 118:24

Try to see each day as an adventure, planned out by Me, your Guide. Instead of trying to make your day into what you want it to be, open your eyes to all the things I have prepared just for you. Each day is My precious gift to you—and you only have one chance to live it. Trust that I am with you every minute, working in your life. And then thank Me for this day—no matter what happens.

Expect surprises! When you live your life with Me, no day will ever be boring or predictable. Don't take the easiest path. Don't just get through the day. Live it! Be willing to follow Me wherever I lead. Even when My way seems scary, the safest place to be is by My side.

READ ON YOUR OWN

1 Peter 2:21

No Need to Pretend

People look at the outside of a person, but the Lord looks at the heart.
—1 Samuel 16:7 (ICB)

Everyone wants to look good. You want to wear the right clothes, fix your hair just so, and say just the right things. It's easy to clean up your outside and make your friends think you have it all together on the inside. You can fool a lot of people that way. But not Me. I see straight through you. I understand who you really are, and *I love you*.

Talk to Me about your struggles, about the times when you feel that you just aren't good enough. Little by little, I will take those struggles and turn them into strengths. You don't have to pretend or put on a show with Me. Just be yourself. There is nothing you can do—or not do—that will stop Me from loving you.

READ ON YOUR OWN

Romans 8:38–39

Don't Look at the Waves

And Peter left the boat and walked on the water to Jesus.
But when Peter saw the wind and the waves, he became afraid
and began to sink. He shouted, "Lord, save me!"
—Matthew 14:29–30 (ICB)

Problems are all around you, like the waves in the ocean. But don't look at the waves. Look at Me, and I will keep you safe. If you look only at the waves—at the problems—you will sink in an ocean of worry and fear. Don't be afraid. Simply call out, "Help me, Jesus!" and I will lift you up—just as I did Peter.

I know that you sometimes worry about what's ahead. The future can be frightening—like gigantic waves just waiting to crash down on you. Trust in Me. I already know the future. By the time those gigantic waves get to you, I will have shrunk them down to a size you can face. And I am always beside you, helping you. The closer you are to Me, the safer you will be.

READ ON YOUR OWN

Hebrews 12:2; Philippians 4:7

Don't Rehearse Your Problems

*Be strong and courageous. Do not be terrified; do not be discouraged,
for the L*ORD *your God will be with you wherever you go.*
—Joshua 1:9

Some days are just hard—a tough test, a fight with a friend, trouble at home. You rehearse it over and over in your mind like the words to a song. But when you rehearse your problems that way, you live them over and over again. You were meant to live through them only once—when they actually happen!

Don't try to figure out how you'll get through this situation on your own. Come to Me, and let Me guide you and give you My Peace. Don't forget that I am always with you. I will give you all the strength and courage you need to face whatever challenges come your way. I will turn your worries and your fears into confidence and trust.

READ ON YOUR OWN

Matthew 11:28–30; Joshua 1:5

No More Boring Days

*Do not worry about anything. But pray and ask God for everything
you need. And when you pray, always give thanks. And God's peace
will keep your hearts and minds in Christ Jesus. The peace that
God gives is so great that we cannot understand it.*
—Philippians 4:6–7 (ICB)

C ome to Me with a thankful heart. I have made this day for you so that you can enjoy My Presence in it. Don't worry about tomorrow. Rejoice in today. Look for the many blessings and miracles that I have put into this day. If you look for My Presence in your life, you will find it.

Come to Me with all your needs, big and small, knowing that I will take care of you. When you are not worried about what is happening in your life, then you are free to truly live. I want to give you that freedom. Turn your heart over to Me, and I will fill it with peace and joy. And there will be no more boring days!

READ ON YOUR OWN

Psalm 118:24; Philippians 4:19

No Shortcuts

The Lord God gives me my strength. He makes me like a deer, which does not stumble. He leads me safely on the steep mountains.
—Habakkuk 3:19 (ICB)

I have planned out a perfect path for your life, and I am leading you along that path. In the distance, you can see the mountaintop. That's our goal. I know that you want to go straight to the top, but don't take shortcuts. Follow Me instead. Shortcuts can take you into dangerous places.

There will be difficulties along the way, for sure. But I will use them to bless you with courage and strength. At times it might even seem that I am leading you away from the goal. Follow Me anyway. I have lovingly planned every inch of your journey.

Hold My hand and walk with Me. When the path gets rocky and steep—when problems get in your way—hold even tighter to My hand. Together we will make it to the top!

READ ON YOUR OWN

John 21:19; 2 Corinthians 4:17

I Am Still Here

When You said, "Seek My face," My heart said to You,
"Your face, LORD, I will seek."
—Psalm 27:8 (NKJV)

When you seek Me, You will find more than you ever dreamed possible. I will replace your worries with peace, and I will shower you with blessings.

I am all that you are searching and hoping for. That empty place inside you? The one you've tried to fill with stuff, and friends, and so many other things? I am the only One who can fill it. Seek Me!

All the stuff and busyness of this world may sometimes distract you and take your attention away from Me. But I am watching and waiting for you to return to Me. And when you do search for Me again, you will find that I am still here with you—right where I have always been.

READ ON YOUR OWN

Philippians 4:7; Jeremiah 29:13

Trust My Way

For just as the heavens are higher than the earth, so my ways are higher than your ways and my thoughts higher than your thoughts.
—Isaiah 55:9 (NLT)

As you start this day, remember that I am in control. As you make plans for the day, remember that I am the One who is really in charge of it.

I am always with you—whether you realize it or not. On days when everything is going smoothly, you may not notice Me at all. But on those days when things don't go as *you* planned—look for Me! I may be doing something important in your life, something very different from what you expected. Don't try to figure out what is happening. Simply trust My way, and thank Me for the great things I am doing in your life.

READ ON YOUR OWN

Isaiah 55:10–11; Jeremiah 29:11

I Will Catch You!

Neither height nor depth, nor anything else in all creation, will be able to separate us from the love of God that is in Christ Jesus our Lord.
—Romans 8:39

I want you to be all Mine. I want you to depend only on Me—not on your friends, or yourself, or your circumstances.

Depending only on Me may make you feel a bit like the tight-rope walker at the circus. But don't be afraid of falling; I am your safety net. I will catch you—I promise! So don't look down. Look ahead to Me. I am always in front of you, encouraging you to come closer to Me, one step at a time. There is nothing in the whole world that can separate you from My Love.

READ ON YOUR OWN

Deuteronomy 33:27

Hidden Blessings

*Trust in the Lord with all your heart and do not lean
on your own understanding. In all your ways acknowledge Him,
and He will make your paths straight.*
—Proverbs 3:5–6 (NASB)

Learn to trust Me in all situations—the tough ones, as well as the easy ones. Trust Me when you don't understand what's going on. Trust Me when everything seems to be spinning out of control. Trust Me when you feel like you are all alone and no one understands. *I understand.*

Don't waste your time thinking about how things should have been. Don't try to run away. Start right this minute—accepting things exactly as they are—and search for My way through your challenges. Learn to look for the blessings and the opportunities I have hidden in those difficulties. Trust Me and lean on Me. I love you, and I will never let you down.

READ ON YOUR OWN

Psalm 52:8

January 23

Shine!

God once said, "Let the light shine out of the darkness!" And this is the same God who made his light shine in our hearts. He gave us light by letting us know the glory of God that is in the face of Christ.
—2 Corinthians 4:6 (ICB)

It's okay to be human. If your mind wanders while you are praying, don't be surprised or upset. Simply turn your thoughts back to Me, and know that I understand.

Don't let your prayer time be the only time you think about Me. Take time for Me throughout your day. Just whisper My Name. Say a simple prayer of thanks. Smile as you think about how much I love you. That is worship. Making these moments of worship a part of your day will create in you a gentle and quiet spirit. And that makes Me very happy.

As you grow closer to Me, the light of My Love will shine through you. Those around you will see it and be blessed.

READ ON YOUR OWN

Deuteronomy 31:6; 1 Peter 3:4;
2 Corinthians 4:6–7; 2 Corinthians 12:9

The Greatest of Treasures

Dear brothers and sisters, when troubles come your way,
consider it an opportunity for great joy.
—James 1:2 (NLT)

My Peace is the greatest of treasures. It is the most expensive of gifts, both for Me the Giver and for you the receiver. I bought this peace for you with My own blood. And to receive it, you must learn to trust Me in the middle of life's storms.

When everything is going your way, you have the peace of this world, and it is easy to forget about Me. But that kind of peace does not last. It cannot handle problems. It can't heal broken hearts, lost friendships, or big disappointments. But My Peace can. It can even find a way to turn troubles into blessings, making you stronger in your faith.

Expect troubles every day. They are just a part of living in an imperfect world. But when they come your way, be glad, for I have overcome this world—and all its troubles.

READ ON YOUR OWN

Matthew 13:46; John 16:33

Sit with Me

Our faces, then, are not covered. We all show the Lord's glory, and we are being changed to be like him. This change in us brings more and more glory. And it comes from the Lord, who is the Spirit.
—2 Corinthians 3:18 (ICB)

Take a moment and just sit quietly with Me. Let My Love surround you and fill you. Feel the Light of My Presence, and enjoy My Peace. I am using these quiet moments to do much more than you can imagine. Give Me this gift of your time, and then watch how I bless you and those you love.

Your friendship with Me is changing you from the inside out. I am shaping you into the person I want you to be. Don't fight the changes, or try to speed them up. Let Me set the pace as I create a better you. Hold My hand and walk with Me—step by step.

READ ON YOUR OWN

Hebrews 13:15; Psalm 73:23–24

Trust Me Anyway

I told you these things so that you can have peace in me. In this world you will have trouble. But be brave! I have defeated the world!
—John 16:33 (ICB)

You might be thinking that you deserve a problem-free life. But that is simply not true. You want an answer to every problem you face. But that will not happen. Just as I told My disciples, in this world you *will* have trouble! If you walk with Me, I won't promise you a problem-free life, but I will promise you a problem-free eternity.

So stop wasting your energy, wishing that everything was perfect. Instead, pour your energy into seeking Me: the Perfect One. I am the Light in a dark world. When everything is going wrong, trust Me with all your heart. When everything seems dark and confusing—that is when My Light shines brightest.

READ ON YOUR OWN

Psalm 112:4, 7

The Right Road

Do not let your hearts be troubled. Trust in God; trust also in me.
—John 14:1

Trust is the golden road that leads straight to heaven. I dare you to walk that road with Me. Take My hand and trust Me to lead you—even when you don't know where you are going. I will keep you safe, and I will keep you on the right road.

If you choose to follow your own road instead of following Me, then your travels will be dangerous ones. Worries will weigh you down until you are too tired to move. Problems will trip you up and cause you to stumble. Troubles will twist the road, and you will become lost with no one to guide you. If that happens, call out to Me. I will clear away all the confusion, and I will put you back on the right road.

READ ON YOUR OWN

John 14:2; Proverbs 3:5–6

My Promise

You can be sure that I will be with you always.
I will continue with you until the end of the world.
—Matthew 28:20 (ICB)

I *will be with you always.* These were the last words I spoke before I returned to heaven. I still make this promise to everyone who will listen.

People see My promise in different ways. Some Christians believe this promise on Sunday mornings, but then they forget about it as soon as the church doors close. Some people are even afraid of the promise, worried that I am constantly judging them. But others know the truth. I am always with you because I love you. I want to be your Light, your Protector, your Peace.

Because I am with you all the time, every moment of your life can be special.

READ ON YOUR OWN

Psalm 139:1–4

Capture Every Thought

We capture every thought and make it give up and obey Christ.
—2 Corinthians 10:5 (ICB)

I have given you an amazing gift—the freedom to choose. You may choose to think about anything you wish. I am asking that you choose to think about Me.

Today, let your goal be to capture every thought and bring it to Me. Wherever your mind wanders, lasso those thoughts and show them to Me. Having anxious thoughts? They shrivel up and disappear when My Light shines on them. Having confused thoughts? My Peace will untangle them. Starting to think you're better than someone else? My unconditional Love will help you see that I love all My children, and so should you. Keep your thoughts focused on Me so that you can enjoy My Peace.

READ ON YOUR OWN

Psalm 8:5; Genesis 1:26–27; Isaiah 26:3

Don't Worship Your Worries

He is safe because he trusts the Lord.
—Psalm 112:7 (ICB)

Worship your worries? That sounds crazy, doesn't it? But whatever you think about the most becomes your god, your idol, the thing you worship. When your worries take on a life of their own and take over your thoughts, you are worshiping your worries.

I want you to break free from your worries. How? By trusting Me. By thinking about Me. By worshiping only Me. No one else knows what goes on inside your mind—not your friends, not your teachers, not even your parents. But *I* know your every thought, so be careful concerning what you choose to think about. I am constantly searching your thoughts for a sign of your trust in Me. When I find that your thoughts are about Me, I rejoice! Choose to think about Me more and more; this will keep you close to Me.

READ ON YOUR OWN

1 Corinthians 13:11

The Best Security System Ever

The Lord is my strength and shield. I trust him, and he helps me.
—Psalm 28:7 (ICB)

I am your Strength and your Shield. Long before you get out of bed each morning, I am there, preparing and planning your day. Instead of wondering what will happen and worrying about how you will handle it, talk to Me about it. I've already got it all figured out. If you ask for My help, My Strength will flow freely into you. You will be strong enough to face whatever comes.

If you start to feel afraid, remember that I am your Shield. I'm not just a piece of cold metal—I am alive, always on the alert. I watch over you every minute, protecting you from both known and unknown dangers. I never sleep; I never take a break; I never get distracted.

Trust yourself to My Strength and My Shield—I am the best security system you'll ever find!

READ ON YOUR OWN

Matthew 6:34; Psalm 56:3–4; Genesis 28:15

FEBRUARY

Seek the LORD and His strength;
seek His face continually.

—Psalm 105:4 (NASB)

February 1

Every Step

For he will order his angels to protect you wherever you go.
—Psalm 91:11 (NLT)

The future is like a huge mountain looming in front of you. Its peaks are spiked with troubles, and its sides are pitted with problems. How can you face something so huge?

The real trouble is not the mountain—it's that you're looking *only* at the mountain. And because you aren't looking at where you're going right now, you stumble on the easy path of today.

I know how much that future mountain worries you. But it may not even be part of our path. You don't know what will happen today, much less tomorrow. I may suddenly turn you away from the mountain or show you an easier path. But I promise that if I ask you to climb that mountain, I will give you everything you need to reach the top. My angels will protect you. And I will be right by your side every step of the way.

READ ON YOUR OWN

Psalm 18:29; Psalm 91:12; 2 Corinthians 5:7

A New Way of Thinking

Do not be shaped by this world.
Instead be changed within by a new way of thinking. Then you will be
able to decide what God wants for you. And you will be able to know
what is good and pleasing to God and what is perfect.
—Romans 12:2 (ICB)

I want to give you a new way of thinking. When you just let your thoughts wander, they tend to wander to your problems. Your mind swirls around and around, trying to solve them. You waste time and energy. Worst of all, your mind is so filled with your problems that you lose sight of Me.

Train your mind to look for Me wherever you are. I want your thoughts to be so filled with Me that you lose sight of your problems. I am all around you. Do you see Me? That bird singing, that smile from a friend, that ray of sunshine peeking through the clouds? I send each one your way. That feeling of safety and peace? That's from Me too. I'm always thinking about you. So think about Me.

READ ON YOUR OWN

Psalm 105:4

February 3

I Am Forever

What, then, shall we say in response to this?
If God is for us, who can be against us?
—Romans 8:31

I am with you and for you. You never have to face anything alone—ever! When you are worried, you are thinking about the things of this world—the things you can see—and you are forgetting about Me. It is easy to be distracted by what you can see, but those things are only temporary. And even though you cannot see Me, I am forever.

Getting rid of your worries is simple: Keep your thoughts on Me. Whisper My Name to remind you that I'm with you. Sing a song of praise. Tell Me that you trust Me. I will get you safely through this day and every day.

This day is a precious gift. Don't waste it worrying about the future. Instead, unwrap the gift of today and enjoy its many blessings with Me by your side. As you open this today-gift fully, you'll find Me!

READ ON YOUR OWN

2 Corinthians 4:18; Genesis 16:13–14

No More Comparisons

May the Lord watch over you and give you peace.
—Numbers 6:26 (icb)

I know that sometimes you doubt yourself. You worry what people think about you. You are afraid that you're not good enough. You think no one cares.

I want you to bring those fears and doubts to Me and let Me give you peace. Accept yourself as the person I created you to be. Don't wear yourself out comparing yourself to others. Instead, be thankful for how I made you, and trust Me as I guide you through this day.

As you learn to live with Me as the Center of your life, My Peace will fill you up. You will stop worrying about how you look and what other people think of you, because you will be too busy living the life I have planned for you.

READ ON YOUR OWN

Psalm 29:11; Numbers 6:24–25; Psalm 13:5

Run to Me

*Therefore we will not fear, though the earth give way
and the mountains fall into the heart of the sea.*
—Psalm 46:2

There are so many things to worry about. Did you study enough for the big test? Did your friend really mean that? Why can't you seem to make your parents understand?

Worry makes you afraid and anxious. But you have a choice, and it's a choice that you will have to make a thousand times every day. You must choose whether to trust Me or to worry. Choose to trust Me, and I will trade your fear for My Peace. Every time you choose Me over worry, I will give you even more of My Peace.

You will never run out of things to worry about. Choose to run to Me instead—I will never run out of Peace.

READ ON YOUR OWN

Romans 8:6; Psalm 46:1

Rest

*Then Jesus said, "Come to me, all of you who are weary
and carry heavy burdens, and I will give you rest."*
—Matthew 11:28 (NLT)

When you're so tired you can hardly stand, doesn't it feel wonderful when you finally get to sink into your own bed? Your body relaxes; your breathing slows; your bones just seem to melt into the mattress. And you rest.

Just as your body gets tired, so does your spirit. Trying to do the right thing can really wear you out sometimes, especially if everyone around you is doing what's wrong. Sometimes you just need a break.

Come to Me. Lift up your hands in prayer to Me. Lie back and rest in My Presence. Take a deep breath of My Peace. I will refresh you and give you the strength to keep going.

READ ON YOUR OWN

Matthew 11:29; 1 Timothy 2:8

February 7

Don't Be Distracted

Why am I so sad? Why am I so upset? I should put my hope in God.
I should keep praising him, my Savior and my God.
—Psalm 42:11 (ICB)

Sometimes things just don't go the way you expect them to, or even the way you think they should. But I have a plan. I also have the Power to take all those unexpected things—even the not-so-good ones—and use them for good in your life.

Your job is pay attention to Me. Let Me guide you through the many choices you face each day. That may sound easy, but it's not. The devil wants your attention too. He knows the things that will distract you from Me—too much television, a game you just can't put down, or a friend who tempts you to make bad choices. The devil tries to trip you up. But it is *My* path that you are on, and I will help you follow it one step, one decision, at a time.

READ ON YOUR OWN

Romans 8:28

I Will Lift You Up

And God raised us up with Christ and seated us with him
in the heavenly realms in Christ Jesus.
—Ephesians 2:6

I am above all things: your problems, your disappointments and hurts, and all the ever-changing events that fill up this world. And I want to lift you above all these things too.

It's a fact: You will have problems in this life. You will stumble and fall into the dirt and dust of this world. But don't give up! Don't let the dirt and dust be the only thing you see. See Me! Reach out your hand and call out, "Help me, Jesus!"

I am always near you. I will grab your hand, and I will pull you up. I will dust you off and sit you beside Me. And I will show you how—together—we can get through it all.

READ ON YOUR OWN

Matthew 14:28–32

February 9

The Treasure Hunt

God is the one who saves me. I trust him. I am not afraid.
—Isaiah 12:2 (ICB)

Did you know that you are on a treasure hunt? It's not a hunt for a prize, a bag of candy, or even a pirate's chest full of gold. It's a hunt for Me. I am the Treasure. I've given you the map of My Holy Word to follow, and I've given you My Spirit to guide you.

The road you must take is not an easy one, but the Treasure is worth it! All along the way, I'm waiting to give you jewels of blessings. Hardships are part of the journey too—just as they are with any great adventure. But don't be afraid; I'm with you. I will give you strength, and I will fill your heart with a joy that will make you sing. And at the end of your journey is the greatest treasure of all—eternity with Me!

READ ON YOUR OWN

Psalm 27:8; 2 Corinthians 4:7

The Ultimate Time Manager

I will instruct you and teach you in the way you should go;
I will counsel you and watch over you.
—Psalm 32:8

There is so much to do—there are so many demands on your time. School. Homework. Practice. Family. Friends. None of these things alone is bad. But together they can make you so busy that you don't feel like you have time for Me.

Don't fall into the trap of being constantly on the go. Don't be too busy for Me. If you will spend time with Me—studying My Word and talking to Me—I will help you sort out what is really important and what is not.

Because I will help you see clearly what you need to do, you will be able to do more in less time. And because I am the all-powerful King of the universe, I can actually bend time and events in your favor, to help you out. I am the *ultimate* Time Manager.

READ ON YOUR OWN

Luke 10:41–42

Dark Days

Think about Jesus. He held on patiently while sinful men were doing evil things against him. Look at Jesus' example so that you will not get tired and stop trying.
—Hebrews 12:3 (ICB)

Some days, everything goes your way. You make the winning shot, ace the big test, say just the right thing to impress your friends. On those days, the sun seems to shine brighter, you walk with a bounce in your step, and My Light blends in with the brightness of your day. You may not even notice Me.

But other days, nothing goes right. You trip and everyone laughs, you blow the test, and you hurt your best friend's feelings. There is no bounce in your step, and your day seems dark. But on those dark days, it's easiest to see My Light shining through.

Dark days are a part of My training program. I am training you to see My Light—no matter how dark your day seems.

READ ON YOUR OWN

John 1:4–5

Your Thoughts
Are Precious to Me

*Take delight in the L*ORD*, and he will give you your heart's desires.*
—Psalm 37:4 (NLT)

I am right here with you, peeking over your shoulder, reading your every thought. Some people say that it doesn't matter what you think, because no one can read your mind. But I can. And your thoughts are precious to Me. When you think about Me and how you love Me, I smile. When you think about others and how you should treat them, I am proud of you.

Commercials, billboards, and magazines all try to tell you what you should think about—the big game, being famous, or getting that new, must-have pair of jeans. These things will make you happy, they say. But that is a lie. I created you, and I alone can bring you true Joy.

READ ON YOUR OWN

Matthew 1:23

I Give You Peace

Jesus said, "Peace be with you!"
—John 20:21

I *give you Peace!* These are the words I have been saying to My followers ever since I rose from the grave. I died like a criminal on the cross, but I did it for you. With My blood, I was able to purchase Peace for you. I wore a crown of thorns so that I could give you a crown of Peace.

How do you get My Peace? It is so simple. Find a quiet place, sit for a moment, think about Me, and thank Me for loving you so much. When you do this, I will come and sit beside you. I will wrap you up in My Peace like a warm blanket. This will keep your heart close to Mine.

READ ON YOUR OWN

John 20:19; John 14:27

Be Bold!

I am the Lord your God. I am holding your right hand.
And I tell you, "Don't be afraid. I will help you."
—Isaiah 41:13 (ICB)

Today is an adventure, and I want you to live it to the fullest. Be bold! Be courageous! I am right there with you every second.

Don't let fear or worry get in your way. They are robbers. They rob you of the exciting and joyful life that I have planned for you. Don't worry about what might go wrong, or what your friends might say. Trust Me enough to face problems as they come, instead of making up problems to worry about. Whenever you start to feel afraid, remember that I am holding your hand. Nothing can separate you from My Presence!

READ ON YOUR OWN

Hebrews 12:2

I Am Your Shepherd

The Lord is my shepherd. I have everything I need.
—Psalm 23:1 (ICB)

A shepherd cares for his sheep. When they are hungry, he leads them to food. When they are thirsty, he finds water. When they are hurt, he takes care of them. When wild animals attack, he protects them. When they are surrounded by the darkness of the night, he comforts them.

I am your Shepherd, and you are My most precious sheep. I am taking care of you, so you don't have to be afraid of anything—ever. Your job is to follow Me. A sheep does not lead the shepherd, so you need to give Me control of your life. Though this may feel scary at times—even dangerous—the safest place to be is right next to Me.

READ ON YOUR OWN

Luke 1:37; Ephesians 3:20–21; Psalm 23:2–4

Still and Quiet

*Be still before the L*ORD*.*
—Zechariah 2:13

It's tough to be still and quiet. There are so many things you could be doing—playing outside, talking to a friend, going to the game. But there are times when you have to be still—when you are sick, when you have finished your classwork, or when others need you to be quiet. Instead of wishing away this time, use it to listen for Me and to thank Me for My Presence in your life.

Some of My greatest work is done when you are still and quiet. That is when you can hear Me whisper to your heart.

READ ON YOUR OWN

Isaiah 30:15; 2 Corinthians 12:9

A New You

Therefore, if anyone is in Christ, he is a new creation;
the old has gone, the new has come!
—2 Corinthians 5:17

I came to earth, was crucified, and then rose from the grave so that I could create a *new you*. A "you" who isn't stuck in a boring routine, who doesn't worry what others think, who isn't afraid to try new things.

I want you to have an exciting life, full of adventure and challenge. I have lots of plans for you; I want you to do great things for My kingdom. First, though, you have to give Me control of your old life. Let Me have your old worries, your old struggles, your old temptations and sins. I will throw them all away so that I can work in your life.

Change can be frightening, but trust Me. I have great plans for this day—and every day—of your life.

READ ON YOUR OWN

Matthew 28:5–7

Count on Me

The LORD your God is with you, he is mighty to save.
—Zephaniah 3:17

No one is perfect—not your best friend, not your mom or your dad, not your sports hero or favorite television star. Sooner or later, someone in your life—someone you really count on—will let you down. You can end up feeling angry, hurt, and betrayed. You may feel like you are falling, with no one to catch you or help you up. So who can you count on?

Count on Me. I will never let you down. And when others do let you down, I will be your safety net. I will not let you crash. Not only am I always there with you, but I am holding your hand. And I promise, I won't ever let go.

READ ON YOUR OWN

Psalm 73:23–26

Break Away

God said to Moses, "I AM WHO I AM."
—Exodus 3:14

There are times when you feel like you are drowning in problems. You feel like you just can't catch a break. There's that math problem you can't seem to figure out, that sports play you can't get right, that family problem that just gets worse and worse. It's all you can think about.

Make yourself break away from the struggles. Go outside and find a quiet place. Take a deep breath and humbly give your thoughts to Me. Remember who I AM in all My Power and Glory. I will shine the Light of My Presence on your problems. I will help you see them as they really are. And I will give you joy, in spite of your troubles. Together we can handle anything.

READ ON YOUR OWN

Habakkuk 3:17–19

I Will Never Disappoint You

Let the peace of Christ rule in your hearts.
—Colossians 3:15

You live in a world that is constantly changing. Nothing—and no one—ever stays the same. The weather changes, you grow taller, your friendships change, your relationship with your parents changes, people move away, interests change . . . and on and on.

Not only does this world change, but it is a world filled with sin. The people around you are going to make mistakes. Your feelings will get hurt. You are going to mess up. If you count on this world—or the people in it—to make you happy and give you peace, sooner or later you will be disappointed.

True, never-ending Peace can come only from Me. Ask Me to fill your heart with My Love and Peace. I will never disappoint you.

READ ON YOUR OWN

Colossians 1:27

February 21

It's Your Choice

As you received Christ Jesus the Lord, so continue to live in him.
Keep your roots deep in him and have your lives built on him.
Be strong in the faith, just as you were taught.
And always be thankful.
—Colossians 2:6–7 (ICB)

*T*rust and *thankfulness*. You hear those words a lot, but why are they so important to Me? Because they are the two things that you must have to stay close to Me.

When you *trust* Me, you are not worrying or trying to fix things yourself. You are keeping your eyes on Me, thinking about Me and what I want for you. When you are *thankful* to Me, there is no room for criticizing or complaining—those sins that can trip you up by tearing down other people.

Trusting and being thankful are choices that only you can make. And you'll have to make them every single day, many times a day. Just as with sports or math or any other skill, the more you practice, the easier it becomes!

READ ON YOUR OWN

Psalm 141:8; 1 Peter 5:7

The Empty Spot

Ask and you will receive. And your joy will be the fullest joy.
—John 16:24 (ICB)

I created you with a need. It is an empty spot inside you. You may try to fill that empty spot with stuff or with friends, or even with sin. It may even work for a short while. But sooner or later, those things will fail you and you will be left feeling even emptier than before. I am the only one who can fill your empty spot.

You need Me every second of every day. And you can reach Me every second of every day. Pray all the time. It doesn't have to be a long prayer or one full of fancy words. Just say a simple, short prayer about whatever is happening at the moment. Let Me know you are thinking about Me. Or simply say My Name. Or whisper to yourself a verse from My Word. Just keep talking to Me; I will always be listening.

READ ON YOUR OWN

1 Thessalonians 5:17

The Pit of Self-Pity

So let us run the race that is before us and never give up.
—Hebrews 12:1 (ICB)

It's easy to feel sorry for yourself—especially when things aren't going your way, or you feel like everyone is against you, or you are just plain tired of trying so hard all the time. But feeling sorry for yourself is one of the devil's favorite traps. Don't even go near it! Once you fall into his trap, it is very hard to get out again.

How can you protect yourself from the devil's traps? Focus on Me. When you are feeling sorry for yourself, you are thinking only about yourself and your problems. But when you think about Me and praise Me for My Presence, then you won't stumble into the pit of self-pity. Stay close to Me in your words and thoughts. I will give you the energy to run the race—and never give up!

READ ON YOUR OWN

Psalm 89:15–16; Hebrews 12:2

I Love You

Now all we can see of God is like a cloudy picture in a mirror.
Later we will see him face to face. We don't know everything,
but then we will, just as God completely understands us.
—1 Corinthians 13:12 (CEV)

I *love you*. Take a moment, be still, and think about that. I am the Creator of the universe, the Ruler of Time, the Master of all that you see—and I love *you*. My Love is so big that it fills up all of space, time, and eternity.

I know that you don't fully understand the hugeness of My Love for you. You see glimpses of it now—as you feel Me guiding you, drawing you closer to Me, and answering your prayers. But one day you will see Me face-to-Face. Then you will know exactly how wide and long and high and deep My Love for you really is. For now, just know that My Love is so huge it cannot be measured. And it goes with you through every moment of every day.

READ ON YOUR OWN

Ephesians 3:16–19

Slow Down!

Give thanks whatever happens.
That is what God wants for you in Christ Jesus.
—1 Thessalonians 5:18 (ICB)

The alarm clock goes off, and you bolt out of bed like a race-horse. You dash to the kitchen, wolf down some breakfast, and then it's out the door. You run, run, run through your day . . .

Slow down! Did you yawn and stretch and thank Me for a healthy body that can get out of bed? Did you peek outside and see that beautiful sunrise I made for you? Did you thank Me for the food you ate? Or the home you live in? Or the people who love you?

Don't be so rushed that you forget to notice the blessings I fill your day with. Stop for a moment. Enjoy. Thank Me. Thankfulness not only pleases Me, but it also protects you from thoughts that make you sad. When you're thankful for the blessings all around you, you feel much happier. So slow down—and give thanks!

READ ON YOUR OWN

Colossians 4:2

The Future Is My Secret

There are some things the Lord our God has kept secret.
—Deuteronomy 29:29 (ICB)

Sometimes you think it might be nice to know the future, what to expect, how things will turn out. There are even some people who claim they can tell you the future. But the future is a secret. It is *My* secret.

When you try to figure out the future, you are reaching for something that is Mine. By keeping your future a secret, I am teaching you to depend on Me. Trust My promises to care for you, to look out for you. I will show you the next step you need to take, and the one after that, and the one after that—one step at a time. Don't try to rush ahead of Me. Just relax and enjoy the journey to your future—one day at a time.

READ ON YOUR OWN

Psalm 32:8

Live This Day

Yet I am always with you; you hold me by my right hand.
—Psalm 73:23

Will you do well on your exam? Will your friend still be angry? Will you live up to what your parents expect from you? I know these kinds of things worry you. But your greatest danger is worrying about tomorrow.

Just as physically you can only carry so many heavy boxes, spiritually you can only carry so many burdens. *Today* is the only day you have to live. If you try to carry tomorrow's worries while you are living today, you will stumble and fall because the load is just too heavy. You must choose to live *this* day. Give your worries about tomorrow to Me, and I will carry them for you. I will be right beside you, holding your hand.

READ ON YOUR OWN

1 Corinthians 10:13

A Jewel in My Crown

The Lord makes me very happy. All that I am rejoices in my God. The Lord has covered me with clothes of salvation. He has covered me with a coat of goodness. I am like a bridegroom dressed for his wedding. I am like a bride dressed in jewels.
—Isaiah 61:10 (ICB)

Stop comparing yourself to other people. When you compare yourself to others, you end up either feeling that you're better than they are, or feeling bad about yourself. Neither of those things is what I want for you.

I created each of My children with unique talents. And I have given each of you your own road to follow. So it is useless to compare yourself to someone else—that person has a completely different path to follow.

When you want to feel good about yourself, remember how much I love you. Remember that I made you just the way I want you to be. And remember that I died so you could have My salvation. You are a jewel in My crown.

READ ON YOUR OWN

Luke 6:37; John 3:16–17; Proverbs 3:11–12

February 29

Follow Me

Jesus answered . . . "You must follow me."
—John 21:22 (cev)

The evil one wants you to follow his path instead of Mine. He will tell you his way is easier—that you can do whatever you want. He will tell you other people don't follow Me, and they seem to do just fine. He will tell you that other kids will laugh at you for following Me.

These are all lies. If you choose his path, you will fall. But he will not help you up; instead, he will hold you down.

I created a path just for you, and I will lead you down it day by day. I will help you over every obstacle. I will pick you up whenever you fall. I will walk alongside you so that you are never alone. Just as I said to My disciple Peter, so I say to you: "Follow Me."

READ ON YOUR OWN

Psalm 119:105

MARCH

When he has led out all of his sheep,
he walks in front of them, and they
follow, because they know his voice.

—John 10:4 (CEV)

I'm Right by Your Side

You, Lord, give true peace. You give peace to those who depend on you.
You give peace to those who trust you.
—Isaiah 26:3 (ICB)

If something in your life is making you anxious, come talk to Me about it. I am your best Friend—the one who always wants to hear from you, no matter what time of day or night it is.

When you pray, tell me what you need and then thank Me. Thank Me for listening. Thank Me for answering. And thank Me for the chance to trust Me more. You see, I use your tough times to make you a better, stronger person.

The world has it backward. The world says if you have enough money, enough stuff, the right friends, then you will have peace and security. But money and stuff can be stolen, and friends can let you down. True peace and security come only from Me. All you have to do is ask—I'm always right by your side.

READ ON YOUR OWN

Philippians 4:6

The Best Life

Jesus said to her, "I am the resurrection and the life.
He who believes in me will live, even though he dies."
—John 11:25

People search for life in all kinds of ways. They spend their time on fun and pleasures. They buy more stuff. They do whatever it takes to be popular, rich, or famous. They chase after things that won't even matter in a few years—and certainly not in eternity.

Meanwhile, I am waiting. Look for *Me*. I am Life! To those who seek Me, I give abundant Life. That means I pour Myself into you—My Joy, My Presence, My Love. I fill you with My purpose and work in this world through you. Not only will your life make a difference on this earth, but also you will build up treasures in heaven. Come to Me, and I will give you the very best life.

READ ON YOUR OWN

Matthew 11:28–29; 1 Peter 1:8–9; Matthew 6:19

Listen for My Voice

His sheep follow him because they know his voice.
—John 10:4

There are lots of voices out there trying to get your attention. Friends, television—and yes, even the devil. They all try to tell you what is important and how you should act. And often, they all say something different. If you listen to all those voices, you will end up running in circles and getting nowhere—like a puppy chasing its tail!

Learn to listen for *My* voice. Learn to tell My voice apart from all the others. How is that possible? *Pray.* Ask My Spirit to help you hear My voice above all the others. Listen closely to what I have to say, and then follow Me wherever I lead.

READ ON YOUR OWN

Ephesians 4:1–6

Worry Worms

Who of you by worrying can add a single hour to his life?
Since you cannot do this very little thing,
why do you worry about the rest?
—Luke 12:25–26

Have you ever seen a worm try to wriggle back into the dirt? That is what worry is like. It is constantly trying to wriggle its way back into your mind.

In this life, there will always be something that you *could* worry about. Something that just isn't quite right. That is part of living in an imperfect world. But worry can't do anything except tie you up into knots.

So how do you get rid of those worry worms? Keep your thoughts on Me. Think about how much I love you, how you can serve Me, and how I bless and protect you. When your mind is all filled up with Me, there's no room for worry worms.

READ ON YOUR OWN

1 Thessalonians 5:16–18

Make Friends with Your Problems

And we know that God causes everything to work together for the good of those who love God and are called according to his purpose for them.
—Romans 8:28 (NLT)

Make friends with the problems in your life. Yes, that's right. And don't forget to thank Me for them either. That sounds crazy, doesn't it? But I can use every single problem to teach you something. Just as a sculptor chisels away bits of rough stone to reveal a beautiful masterpiece, I can use your problems to chip away rough bits of stubbornness, pride, and selfishness to reveal My masterpiece—you!

It's your choice. You can keep your problems all to yourself, so that they grow and become stumbling blocks that trip you up. *Or* you can make friends with your problems by introducing them to Me and letting Me make them part of My plan. I may not take your problems away, but I will make something good come out of them.

READ ON YOUR OWN

1 Corinthians 1:23–24

I Am Always

So he is always able to save those who come to God through him.
He can do this, because he always lives, ready to help those
who come before God.
—Hebrews 7:25 (ICB)

I am the Creator and Ruler of time and space. I am not subject to the same limitations that you are. I am able to be everywhere at every time.

I have always been with you. I know every struggle and every success that you have ever had. I am right here with you now, helping you through this day. And I go on ahead of you into the future, so that I know what is coming in your life and I can prepare you for it. I am *always*. I can be in yesterday, today, and tomorrow—and still never let go of your hand.

READ ON YOUR OWN

Psalm 37:3–4

March 7

Don't Go It Alone

You are my help. Because of your protection, I sing.
I stay close to you. You support me with your right hand.
—Psalm 63:7–8 (ICB)

It is a simple fact: You cannot make it by yourself. More importantly, you don't *have* to make it by yourself. It's up to you.

Yes, there will be days when everything goes just the way you planned. You've got everything under control, and you are living on top of the world. But then—BAM! Trouble—*big* trouble—comes and yanks away the control you thought you had. An illness, an accident, it's something you never saw coming.

You know you need help. Let Me help you. I already know the answers. Let Me guide you to them. But first you have to choose: Do you stubbornly go it alone? Or do you humbly come to Me and let Me help you? Please, choose Me.

READ ON YOUR OWN

James 1:2–3

Seek Me First

But seek first his kingdom and his righteousness,
and all these things will be given to you as well.
—Matthew 6:33

I know that you have goals—some big and some small, some just for today and some for your whole life. I want you to talk with Me about each of these goals. Don't just dive headlong into what you want to do and then ask Me to bless it. When you are determined to get your own way, you leave Me out.

Talk with Me first. Let Me help you see things from My point of view. If your goal fits My plan for your life, I will help you reach it. If it is against My plan for you, I will slowly change your heart so that you will come to want what I want. Seek Me first, and the rest of your life will fall into place, piece by piece.

READ ON YOUR OWN

1 Chronicles 16:11

I Make You Complete

But the fruit of the Spirit is love, joy, peace, patience, kindness,
goodness, faithfulness, gentleness and self-control.
—Galatians 5:22–23

This world moves so fast—and not just cars, jet planes, and rocket ships. People and events move fast. *You're* expected to move fast. There are so many things you're supposed to do, so many places to go, so many people demanding your attention. Like riding too long on a merry-go-round, it can make you dizzy and leave you feeling empty inside.

When everything is spinning too fast, come to Me. I will stop the spinning.

The world says it can make you whole and complete—just *do* this, or *be* that. But the world only takes; it doesn't give back. Only I can make you whole. I can fill up the emptiness with My Love, Joy, and Peace. You will be complete—and then you can help others find Me too.

READ ON YOUR OWN

1 John 4:12

You Are Safe

The ways of God are without fault. The Lord's words are pure.
He is a shield to those who trust him.
—Psalm 18:30 (ICB)

Y ou are mine for all time—beyond time and into eternity. I will never let go of your hand. And nothing can take you out of My hand. You are completely safe with Me.

Because you know that your future is secure, you can live fully today. Don't see today as a blank page that you need to fill up. Live it! I have lovingly and carefully planned this day for you. I have paid attention to every detail—big and small. Be on the lookout for all that I am doing. Talk to Me throughout the day. Ask Me to show you the wonders of this day. It sounds easy, but to do it, you have to trust Me deeply. Trust that you are safe and that My way is the perfect way.

READ ON YOUR OWN

Psalm 37:23–24

March 11

Step Out

Since we live by the Spirit, let us keep in step with the Spirit.
—Galatians 5:25

It's easy to look at all the things you have to do today—school, chores, homework, practice—and say, "I just can't do any more." You want to do good things for Me, but you feel over-whelmed and exhausted by all the other tasks of your day. But remember that you don't have to rely on your own strength. Reach out to Me and I will help you. Let Me give you My Strength and My energy, which never run out.

Be brave! Step out in faith, and I will step right out with you. Let Me work through you. Together we will do great things for My kingdom.

READ ON YOUR OWN

2 Corinthians 5:7

Three Little Words

Wait for the Lord's help.
Be strong and brave and wait for the Lord's help.
—Psalm 27:14 (ICB)

Trust. Wait. Hope. These three little words are all connected—
and they also connect you to Me.

Your faith begins with *trust*. Each day, choose to trust Me and My
way more than you trust yourself. Trust Me to be there for you,
to care for you, and to keep My promises.

Then, *wait* on Me. I will answer your prayers, but it will be in My
own perfect time. If you say, "I trust you," but you keep trying to
make things happen right away, then you are not really trusting
Me. Real trust means *waiting* for My answer.

But wait with *hope*. Don't just wish for My answer; expect it!
Expect to live a life full of meaning and purpose. Expect your
heavenly reward.

Trust. Wait. Hope. Three little words—three keys to My kingdom.

READ ON YOUR OWN

John 14:1; Hebrews 6:18–20

A Joy No One Can Steal

Now you are sad. But I will see you again and you will be happy.
And no one will take away your joy.
—John 16:22 (ICB)

Y ou will have troubles. There will be sadness and hardship and hurt. But do not let these things take over your life. Don't let them be all that you think about. Learn to live above your troubles.

How is that possible? Through Me. When you spend a few minutes every day just sitting quietly with Me, I can give you the power to face your problems with a smile. You will begin to see your struggles as I see them. I will help you decide what is important and what is not. And I will fill your mind with Peace and Joy that no one can take away from you. I have already overcome the troubles of this world, and I will help you do the same with your problems.

READ ON YOUR OWN

John 16:33

My Gift to You

*And I pray that you and all God's holy people will have
the power to understand the greatness of Christ's love.
I pray that you can understand how wide and how long
and how high and how deep that love is.*
—Ephesians 3:18 (ICB)

In this world, you work for what you get. You study hard to get a good grade. You practice hard so you can start in the next game. You work hard at home so your parents will let you hang out with your friends. The harder you work, the more you get.

Maybe that's why what I have to offer seems too good to be true. You can't work for it, because salvation is a free gift. I also *give* you Love, Joy, Peace, and so much more. I'm pleased when I see you working for My kingdom, but you cannot earn My gifts. You can only accept them. I offer them to you because I love you. And My Love is wider and longer and higher and deeper than you could ever imagine.

READ ON YOUR OWN

Ephesians 2:8–9; 2 Corinthians 3:18; Ephesians 3:19

Hear My Song

*The L*ord* your God is with you . . . he will rejoice over you with singing.*
—Zephaniah 3:17

D o you hear that? I am singing you a song. It is a love song. You give Me so much joy that I just have to sing!

You won't hear My song like you would a song on the radio. But listen with your heart, and you'll hear Me. I know there is noise all around you. Voices pulling you this way and that way. Don't listen to them! Take a break from all the noise. Find a quiet place to be still in My Presence and listen to My voice.

That beautiful bird's song? It's saying I love you. That whisper of wind through the trees? It's singing My Joy that you are with Me. Even the patter of the rain says you delight Me. Listen to My song—it's like no other music you'll ever hear.

READ ON YOUR OWN

Psalm 46:10; Matthew 7:7

Lighten Up!

A happy heart is like good medicine.
But a broken spirit drains your strength.
—Proverbs 17:22 (ICB)

Lighten up! Share a laugh with Me!

You thought you would never hear Me say that, but I love to laugh. After all, I created laughter! Look at some of the animals I made—monkeys, giraffes, zebras, and camels. Can you see now that I like to laugh, to be creative, to have fun?

Don't take yourself so seriously. It's okay to make a mistake. Everyone stumbles and falls. Everyone does something embarrassing sometimes. Learn to laugh at yourself, and don't worry if other people laugh along. Besides, You have Me on your side, so what are you worried about?

Go ahead, share a joke with Me. Clown around a bit—and we'll have a laugh together.

READ ON YOUR OWN

Philippians 4:13

I Understand You Completely

O LORD, you have examined my heart and know everything about me.
—Psalm 139:1 (NLT)

When you need someone who understands, come to Me. I understand you better than you understand yourself. No detail of your life is hidden from Me. But don't be afraid of that. When I see you—even your mistakes—I see you through the eyes of My grace. This means that I love you, no matter what.

Let the Light of My Love shine deep inside you—let it heal all your hurts and wash away all the bad thoughts and feelings. My forgiveness is always there for you. That is why I died on the cross.

So when no one else seems to understand—come to Me. Enjoy being with the One who understands you completely and loves you perfectly. I will never leave you—no matter what.

READ ON YOUR OWN

Psalm 139:2–4; 2 Corinthians 1:21–22; Joshua 1:5

Don't Get Caught in a Worry-Web

So don't worry about tomorrow. Each day has enough trouble of its own. Tomorrow will have its own worries.
—Matthew 6:34 (ICB)

T rust Me . . . one day at a time. I understand this can be hard to do, especially if you are hurting. That is why I have sent My Spirit to help you. My Spirit is your tutor, living inside you and teaching you to trust Me. Take time to be still and learn from Him. Listen for His quiet voice and His gentle advice.

Trusting Me is something you *choose* to do. When you worry about today and worry about tomorrow, those worries can crisscross in your mind. They create a web of worries that tangle up your thoughts and leave you confused. Don't get caught in that web. Trust Me to take care of you today *and* tomorrow.

READ ON YOUR OWN

Psalm 84:12

I Speak to You in Love

Therefore, there is now no condemnation
for those who are in Christ Jesus.
—Romans 8:1

This world is full of voices. Often they are harsh and hurtful. They say, "You should have done better"; "You really messed up this time"; and "You just don't have what it takes." They can crush you and make you feel worthless.

These voices are not from Me. Even when you make a mistake, I don't reject you or shame you. I speak words of love and forgiveness. I lift you up and tell you the truth. And the truth is that you *do* have what it takes, because I live in you.

Listen to My voice and then let Me speak through you. When you find yourself in a tough situation, pause for a minute and let Me give you the words to say. Hasty words leave no room for Me. Let Me use your words to lift up those around you.

READ ON YOUR OWN

Romans 8:2; Colossians 1:27; 1 Corinthians 6:19

The Gift of the Spirit

This is what God made us for. And he has given us the Spirit
to be a guarantee for this new life.
—2 Corinthians 5:5 (ICB)

I shower blessings down on you every day. Even when you don't notice them, they are there.

One of my greatest blessings is the gift of the Holy Spirit. He lives within you, teaching and guiding you.

The Holy Spirit is like a great multiplier. In math, five plus five equals ten. But five *times* five equals twenty-five—a much bigger result. The Holy Spirit works in much the same way. He takes your faith and multiplies it. You may start with a small bit of faith in Me, but the Spirit works to multiply it so that it grows much greater.

Be sure to thank Me for the gift of My Spirit. This helps Him to work more freely in you, making you even *more* thankful—and more joyful too!

READ ON YOUR OWN

2 Corinthians 3:17; Psalm 50:14

Don't Be Afraid

The LORD, the LORD, is my strength and my song;
he has become my salvation.
—Isaiah 12:2

Don't be afraid. I am your Strength and your Song. I am your Power and your Joy.

What does it mean to have Me as your Strength? I simply spoke and the universe was created! Mountains soared up out of the earth! The sun and stars lit up the sky! My Power is absolutely unlimited. And I am able to take that same Power and make you strong.

Think of it: I am on your side. I will guide you, protect you, and even fight for you if necessary. So don't let yourself become filled up with fear. Fear only blocks My Strength. Instead of being afraid, trust Me—remember that I am your Strength!

I am also your Song. I want you to grab hold of My Joy. Celebrate! Shout for joy because I am right beside you! Sing with Me as we journey together toward heaven!

READ ON YOUR OWN

Isaiah 12:2–3; Psalm 21:6

A Joyful Heart

Rejoice in the Lord always. I will say it again: Rejoice!
—Philippians 4:4

Rejoice! To rejoice in Me is to praise Me with joy and thankfulness. I love to hear you rejoicing. You can sing it. You can shout it. You can whisper it softly—or even pray silently. It doesn't matter *how* you do it; it matters only *that* you do it! Make this a new habit in your life.

When you rejoice in Me, I am lifted up—and I lift you up as well. Rejoicing tells Me that you know your blessings come from Me, and this makes Me want to bless you even more. I do My greatest works through people who have joyful, thankful hearts. So rejoice in Me always. In every situation. As you practice this habit of praise, your life will get better and better!

READ ON YOUR OWN

Psalm 95:1–2; Psalm 9:10

I Never Run Out

I will bless her with plenty of food. I will fill her poor with food.
—Psalm 132:15 (icb)

I am the God of everything—both big and small. I am the God of the mountain and the pebble, the ocean and the puddle. Nothing is too big—or too small—for Me. So when you pray to Me, pray about the big and the small. I *love* to hear you pray about whatever is on your mind. The more you pray, the more answers you will get from Me. And your faith will be strengthened as you see My many answers in your life.

Because I am *infinite*—with no beginning and no end—I never run out of time, out of love, mercy, or forgiveness. I never run out of answers to your prayers. So come to Me with a thankful heart, expecting to receive all that you need. Then watch how I shower you—My beloved child—with blessings.

READ ON YOUR OWN

Psalm 36:7–9; John 6:12–13

I Won't Let You Down

Jesus Christ is the same yesterday and today and forever.
—Hebrews 13:8

There will come a time when you need to let go of someone or something. Perhaps it will be a friend who has turned her back on you, or someone you love who has passed away. Or perhaps it will be your own desire to be in charge of your life. Letting go means trusting that you will be okay without that person or thing in your life.

How can you let go? You have to trust Me—more than you trust what you are trying to let go of. Trust Me more than friends and family, more than stuff, and more than yourself.

How is that possible? Because I am the same yesterday, today, and forever. I don't get sick. I don't move away. I don't get too busy or distracted. And I don't let you down—ever.

READ ON YOUR OWN

Psalm 89:15; Isaiah 41:13

No Grumbling, Please

And do not grumble.
—1 Corinthians 10:10

Grumbling and complaining are not what I want from you. When you grumble, you are telling Me that you don't like the way things are going in your life—that you hate My way of doing things. And when you complain, you are showing an ungrateful heart.

Thankfulness is your protection against the sins of grumbling and complaining. Being thankful also keeps you close to Me. So—when you have too much homework, when your parents give you an extra chore, or when I've said "not now" to one of your prayers—don't grumble or mumble under your breath. Instead, *thank Me* for the things that upset you. Before you know it, you will start to see those things differently. And you'll start to feel better too.

READ ON YOUR OWN
1 Corinthians 10:10; Hebrews 12:28–29;
1 Thessalonians 5:18

While You Wait

It is good to wait quietly for the Lord to save.
—Lamentations 3:26 (ICB)

W aiting is not an easy thing to do, but there is a lot of it in this world. You wait for birthdays to come; you wait for your ride to arrive; you wait in all kinds of lines. You even sometimes wait with worry for bad things that never happen.

Waiting on Me is different. You are waiting for the perfect timing of My plans in your life. Waiting on Me means trusting Me with every fiber of your being instead of trying to figure it all out yourself. When you trust Me—when you wait for My timing—I will fill your life with blessings. I will give you strength and joy and hope. And I will give you My Presence—while you wait.

READ ON YOUR OWN

Lamentations 3:24–25; Isaiah 40:31; Psalm 16:11

I Am the Greatest Blessing

Yet I hold this against you: You have forsaken your first love.
—Revelation 2:4

Don't come to Me just for what I can give you. Anything can become an idol if it distracts you from Me—even My blessings. I do love to give you good things, but the greatest blessing I can give you is *Myself*. I want to be your First Love. Don't let yourself be distracted by anything else—not even my blessings.

When the strongest desire of your heart is to live close to Me, I am filled with joy and you are safe from the danger of idols. So don't skimp on your time with Me. Pray. Study My Word. Think about who I am and how I work in your life. Yes, enjoy My many blessings. But don't forget the greatest blessing of all: having Me in your life!

READ ON YOUR OWN

Romans 12:2; Colossians 1:27

Like a Little Child

I tell you the truth. You must accept the kingdom of God
as a little child accepts things, or you will never enter it.
—Mark 10:15 (ICB)

Sometimes you hear people say, "I wish you would grow up!" But I have a different message for you: "Keep trusting Me— *like a little child.*"

Small children trust Me so easily. They hear the song "Jesus Loves Me," and they believe every single word, without question. But as you grow up, the world tries to pull you away from trusting Me. It wants you to trust money, or stuff, or just doing whatever feels right to you. Don't give in to the world.

I have so much that I want to give you. I poured out My Life on the cross so that I could give you forgiveness and a home in heaven. And all I ask is that you trust Me—like a little child.

READ ON YOUR OWN

Philippians 2:17; Isaiah 26:3

Everything in Its Own Time

There is a time for everything,
and a season for every activity under heaven.
—Ecclesiastes 3:1

Stop trying to work things out before their time has come. You can't take Friday's math test on Thursday. You can't celebrate your August birthday in June. And you can't make My will happen before the right time.

Accept that you must live one day at a time. When something pops into your mind, take a moment to ask Me whether it's part of My plan for you today—or not. If it isn't, trust Me to take care of it. Then forget about it, and concentrate on what you need to do *today*.

Your life will be much less complicated and confusing. There is a time for everything—and I will help you do everything I want you to do, in its own time.

READ ON YOUR OWN

John 16:33

I Will Take Care of You

The everlasting God is your place of safety.
His arms will hold you up forever.
—Deuteronomy 33:27 (ICB)

Trust Me with all your heart. When you get out of bed in the morning, trust Me. At school, trust Me. With your friends, trust Me. When you go to bed each night, trust Me. Trust Me at all times and in every situation. I *will* take care of you. I already have your life perfectly planned out.

When everything around you seems to be going wrong, and you are just tired of trying, whisper these four words: "I trust You, Jesus." When you say this, you stop trying to fix everything your-self, and you trust the plan I have for you. Let Me take care of you. Fall back into the safety of My powerful arms—I promise I'll catch you.

READ ON YOUR OWN

Proverbs 3:5; Jeremiah 29:13–14

I Am Always Good

*Taste and see that the L*ORD *is good;*
blessed is the man who takes refuge in him.
—Psalm 34:8

I am good; there is no bad in Me. None at all. Not even a tiny drop. And the better you get to know Me, the more you will be able to trust in My goodness.

I have a wonderful plan for your life. But you may not always understand that plan. Sometimes My blessings come to you in mysterious ways: even through pain and trouble. I use tough times to teach you more about Me. I can use trouble at home to help you find peace and comfort in Me. I can use a disappointment to teach you that there is joy in My Presence. And I can even use an illness to teach you to be still and listen for My voice.

You won't always understand, but you can learn to trust that I am *always* good.

READ ON YOUR OWN

1 John 1:5; John 20:19; Colossians 3:15

APRIL

Seek his will in all you do, and he will show you which path to take.

—Proverbs 3:6 (NLT)

April 1

Yes, Everything

Pray continually.
—1 Thessalonians 5:17

I am waiting to hear from you. Tell Me about every detail of your day. I want to know what happened at home and at school, and how you felt about it. The big stuff, the little stuff, even the crazy stuff that you just don't understand. I want to be that best Friend you just can't wait to talk to.

Remember, I don't expect you to do everything perfectly. What I do expect is that you will come to Me in prayer about everything—*yes, everything*—that happens in your life. The good stuff, the bad stuff, the stuff you would never tell anyone else.

A great day is not just one in which everything goes your way. A truly great day is one in which you stay in touch with Me. Talk to Me, and My Spirit will guide you every minute, every step of the way.

READ ON YOUR OWN

Proverbs 3:6

Getting Rid of the Weeds

These little troubles are getting us ready for an eternal glory
that will make all our troubles seem like nothing.
—2 Corinthians 4:17 (CEV)

I promise to meet all your needs. And while you may not realize it, your greatest need is for My Peace.

I am the Gardener of your heart, planting seeds of peace. But the world also tosses in seeds. These seeds grow into weeds of pride, worry, and selfishness. If these weeds aren't ripped out quickly, they will choke out all your peace.

I get rid of those weeds in different ways. Sometimes, when you sit quietly in prayer, My Light shines on the weeds and they shrivel up. But other times, I use troubles to encourage you to trust Me. And that trust kills the weeds.

So thank Me for troubles, as well as joys. Because I use them both to make your heart My garden of Peace.

READ ON YOUR OWN

Philippians 4:19

April 3

Don't Be Tricked

Things that are seen don't last forever, but things
that are not seen are eternal. That's why we keep our minds
on the things that cannot be seen.
—2 Corinthians 4:18 (CEV)

In Me, you have everything. In Me, you are whole and complete. It is not possible for you to have a need that I cannot meet. After all, I created you. I created this world and everything in it. Everything is under my control—even when it doesn't look like it.

Sometimes it seems that the bad guys win; that good people suffer for no reason; that evil is the easier way, maybe even the better way. But that is just what the devil wants you to think. He is the great trickster. Don't let him trick you. The things you see are of this world, but they only last for a while. The things you don't see—faith, hope, and love—are the most important things, and they last forever.

READ ON YOUR OWN

1 Corinthians 13:13; Ephesians 3:20

Shhh . . . Be Still

He makes me to lie down in green pastures;
He leads me beside the still waters.
—Psalm 23:2 (NKJV)

I come to you when you are still and quiet. It is then that you can hear Me speaking to your heart.

Don't be discouraged if it is hard to find a quiet time and place. This world likes everything to be loud and fast. Try slipping out into the backyard and letting the sounds of My creation draw you to Me. Shut the door to your room, and close out the world for a while. Turn off the music, and tune in to Me.

My eyes are always on the lookout for a heart that is seeking Me. And that person is so very precious to Me. I know when you are trying to find Me, and My heart is blessed by your efforts.

READ ON YOUR OWN

Zechariah 2:13; 2 Chronicles 16:9; Psalm 23:3

April 5

I Am Waiting

In repentance and rest is your salvation,
in quietness and trust is your strength.
—Isaiah 30:15

I created your body to live in this world—to breathe, to run, and to rest. But I also designed you to be filled with the things of heaven—My Love, My Joy, and My Peace.

No matter how many mistakes you make, I am always waiting to fill you with My Spirit. In fact, when you are full of sadness for something you have done, that is when My Light can shine brightest in your life.

Spend some time alone with Me each day. Give Me all your cares, worries, and sadness. My Spirit will fill you with strength and confidence as you trust Me and walk in My ways.

READ ON YOUR OWN

2 Corinthians 4:7

Open Your Eyes

I will offer you a sacrifice to show how grateful I am, and I will pray.
—Psalm 116:17 (CEV)

I want your *sacrifice* of thanksgiving. But what does that mean? It means that I want you to put aside your favorite show, your MP3 player, your free time—and choose Me instead. I want you to put aside what you want for yourself for a while so that you can spend time with Me.

A sacrifice of *thanksgiving* also means that you are thankful, *no matter what*. If you choose to see only what is wrong, or what is making you unhappy, then your mind will be filled with dark thoughts. If you refuse to enjoy life until that problem is "fixed," you will miss out on My daily blessings of sunshine, flowers, friends—of life and salvation.

Come to Me with a thankful heart—always! Yes, even when something is wrong. Let My Light open your eyes to see the blessings I pour out upon you—day after day after day.

READ ON YOUR OWN

Genesis 3:2–6; 1 John 1:7

April 7

I Am the Potter

*Yet, O L*ord*, you are our Father. We are the clay,
you are the potter; we are all the work of your hand.*
—Isaiah 64:8

Have you ever watched a potter form a piece of art from a lump of clay? Before the potter even begins to shape the clay, he has a plan in mind. It will be a bowl, a vase, a pitcher. He knows exactly what he is going to make and how he is going to use the finished piece. Every detail is formed with love.

You are My clay, and I am your Potter. Before the world was made, I designed you. I have a plan for you in My kingdom. You will be an encourager, a good friend, a sharer of My Word. I shape every day, every event of your life, with Love.

As you go through your day, talk to Me. Let Me show you how this day—with all its joys and troubles—can shape you into the masterpiece I designed you to be.

READ ON YOUR OWN

Psalm 27:8

I Never Left

I am with you and will watch over you wherever you go.
—Genesis 28:15

I am always with you and for you. *Always*. The question is whether or not you are with Me and for Me.

I never leave you. But you leave Me when you ignore Me and refuse to spend time with Me. You leave Me when you say and do things that you know are wrong. You leave Me when you choose being popular over being My child.

So when you can't feel My Presence, know that you are the one who has moved away. I never left. My Love for you is the same yesterday, today, and always. When you feel like I am far away, just whisper My Name. It's a simple act of faith, but it opens your heart to Me. Bring Me your words of love and praise—and then let Me love you!

READ ON YOUR OWN

Romans 8:31; Hebrews 13:8

April 9

Don't Practice Your Problems

The LORD replied, "My Presence will go with you,
and I will give you rest."
—Exodus 33:14

E verywhere you go, I go. Nothing can separate you from My
Love. I love you so much that I even gave My Life for you. You
can trust Me to take care of you.

Sometimes, though, when you aren't really focusing on Me, you
start to rehearse and practice your problems—going over them
again and again in your mind. What will you do about that grade,
this friendship, or that temptation? You start to feel alone and
worried. Then you try to fix it yourself.

But you are *never* alone, because My Presence goes with you
wherever you go. There is no need to worry, and you don't have
to fix anything by yourself. Bring your problems to Me. In My
Presence, many problems simply vanish, and others become
much easier to handle.

Don't practice your problems; practice bringing your problems
to Me.

READ ON YOUR OWN

Romans 8:38–39

I Will Give You Wings

*Blessed is the man who trusts in the L*ORD.
—Jeremiah 17:7

Trust Me with every detail of your life. Yes, trust Me with your life, your salvation—all the really big things. But also trust Me with your friendships, with your hopes and dreams, even with your choices about what to wear and do. Nothing is too big or too small for me. After all, I am the Creator of both Mount Everest and the tiniest grain of sand.

You are safe with Me. Bring Me your mistakes; I won't laugh at you. Bring Me your sins; I won't keep reminding you of them. I am here to forgive you, to encourage you, and to love you. Nothing is wasted when you bring everything to Me. My grace can transform even your sins and mistakes into something wonderful—much like I transform a caterpillar into a magnificent butterfly. Trust Me with everything, and I will give you "wings" to soar through your life.

READ ON YOUR OWN

Romans 8:28; Psalm 40:2; 1 Peter 2:9

Just Today

Forgetting what is behind and straining toward what is ahead,
I press on toward the goal to win the prize for which God has
called me heavenward in Christ Jesus.
—Philippians 3:13–14

I have made this day for you. Be careful not to complain about anything in it—not your English test, not your frizzy hair, not even the weather—because I am the Creator of this day. Instead, *decide* to be happy today. Open your eyes, and choose to look for all the blessings I have hidden in this day.

Then live today—*just today*. Don't think about mistakes you've made in the past. Don't worry about what will happen tomorrow. You will only end up wasting today. I want you to enjoy abundant Life in My Presence—today!

READ ON YOUR OWN

Psalm 118:24

Choose to Trust Me

But I trust in you, O LORD; I say, "You are my God."
—Psalm 31:14

Trusting Me is a choice you must make every minute. It isn't enough to trust Me just sometimes. Again and again throughout the day, you must choose to trust Me. Even many grown-ups don't understand this.

Remember Moses and the Israelites? They had just escaped Egypt. They had seen ten miraculous plagues. They had seen the waters of the Red Sea parted, and they had walked through the sea on dry land. They had seen Pharaoh's army destroyed in the sea. They trusted Me—until they got hungry or thirsty. Then they forgot to trust.

Don't you do the same thing sometimes? When everything is going great, it's easy for you to trust Me. But when things start to go wrong, trusting isn't so easy. It's a choice you have to make. Choose to trust Me all the time.

READ ON YOUR OWN

Exodus 15:22–25

Ordinary Days

I am the vine; you are the branches.
If a man remains in me and I in him, he will bear much fruit;
apart from me you can do nothing.
—John 15:5

Some of your days are full of action, adventure, and challenge. Other days are . . . well, ordinary. But don't let yourself be bored. Choose to be thankful for quiet days, and then use them to spend extra time with Me.

Invite Me into your everyday tasks. Do everything as if you were doing it for Me . . . yes, even making the bed, finishing up your homework, and all the other ordinary stuff of life. And through it all, enjoy simply being in My company.

When you go through the activities of your day side-by-side with Me, My Life becomes woven together with yours. This means you and I are so closely connected that My own Life flows into you—and through you into the world around you. And that is the real secret of having a joy-filled life—even on ordinary days.

READ ON YOUR OWN

Colossians 3:23; Psalm 105:4

Hints of Heaven

We have this hope as an anchor for the soul, firm and secure.
It enters the inner sanctuary behind the curtain.
—Hebrews 6:19

Did you know that you can get a glimpse of heaven right now, here on earth? When you walk along your life-path with Me, you are already experiencing the most important part of heaven—nearness to Me. And all throughout your day, you can find hints of heaven along your pathway.

The morning sunlight that opens your eyes can remind you that in heaven there is no darkness; there is only the Light of My Presence. The birds teach you how to sing My praises—loud and strong and filled with joy. The flowers, the trees, and the skies can all give you glimpses of the beauty that is waiting for you in heaven.

As you walk through your day today, keep your eyes and ears fully open. Hints of heaven are all around you!

READ ON YOUR OWN

1 Corinthians 15:20–23

April 15

I Will Shelter You

I long to dwell in your tent forever and take refuge
in the shelter of your wings.
—Psalm 61:4

Some days just feel out of control. Your regular routine is all messed up. You feel as though you're running in three different directions all at the same time. And you're not really sure what is expected of you. I know that you feel safer when life is predictable, when everything goes as planned. But don't be afraid. Trust Me.

Come to Me and let Me shelter you under My wings. You are completely safe with Me. Put aside your fears and worries. Remember, I can use crazy days to do wonderful things in your life. You may have a chance to do something for Me that wouldn't have happened on an ordinary day. So instead of complaining about an out-of-control day, say *yes* to what I am doing in your life.

READ ON YOUR OWN

Isaiah 12:2; Psalm 61:2–3; 2 Corinthians 3:18

Even When You Don't Understand

And they were calling to one another:
*"Holy, holy, holy is the L*ORD *Almighty;*
the whole earth is full of his glory."
—Isaiah 6:3

Every day, every minute, every second, I want you to be filled with thankfulness—not with complaining. I am the Creator and the Controller of all the universe. Heaven and earth are filled with My Glory.

When you complain, you are saying that you think you could run the world better than I do. Things will happen that you don't understand. You ask "why?" and "why not?" But you do not know all the things that I know. You can only see today. I can see yesterday, today, and forever—all at the same time. I know how everything fits together.

Have faith in Me and trust that I will take care of you. Be thankful and praise Me—even when you don't understand.

READ ON YOUR OWN

Hebrews 13:8; 2 Corinthians 5:7; 1 Thessalonians 5:18

My Training Program

I will make you strong and will help you.
I will support you with my right hand that saves you.
—Isaiah 41:10 (ICB)

Y ou are in training, and I am your Coach. I am training you to keep your thoughts on Me.

You live in a world filled with sights and sounds. Some are good, and some are bad. But I don't want even the good things to take your attention away from Me.

This kind of focus takes training—just like practicing for a sport or a spelling bee. Just as some days you're in a zone where you almost can't miss a shot or misspell a word, some days your thoughts are on Me. Other days, nothing goes right, and every little thing distracts you from Me.

Don't let this throw you. When something grabs your attention, that's okay. Talk to Me about it. If it's a good thing, we'll rejoice together. If it's a problem, we'll work it out together. The key is *together*. When you're together with Me, you will have My Peace.

READ ON YOUR OWN

Psalm 112:7

Peace for Today

Let us then approach the throne of grace with confidence, so that we may receive mercy and find grace to help us in our time of need.
—Hebrews 4:16

When Moses and the Israelites were wandering in the desert, they were given manna to eat. Each morning they gathered just enough for that day. They could not store it for the future. This day-by-day gathering helped them remember that they needed Me—every day.

My Peace works in much the same way. When you come to Me in prayer with a thankful heart, I give you enough Peace for today. I will not give you enough for tomorrow—only today. That is because I want you to come to Me again tomorrow—and each day after that.

If I gave you enough Peace to last your whole life, you might fall into the trap of thinking you didn't need Me. I designed you to need Me every minute. So come to Me every day with a thankful attitude, knowing that I will give you Peace for today.

READ ON YOUR OWN

Exodus 16:14–20; Philippians 4:6–7, 19

No Matter What

Let your face shine on your servant; save me in your unfailing love.
—Psalm 31:16

D o you know that uneasy, twisty feeling you get in the pit of your stomach when you have to give a speech? Or you're up at bat? Or you're next in the dance recital? You worry if you'll be good enough, and if people will like your performance.

Sometimes you can even get that uneasy, twisty feeling about Me. You wonder if you are doing enough to be worthy of My Love. Well, the answer is no. It doesn't matter how great you act or how many things you do to serve Me, you can never be *worthy* of My Love. No one can. But that's the greatest thing about My Love—you don't *have* to be worthy. It's a gift—free and clear. You don't have to earn it. You just have to accept it.

So relax. Do the best you can. And know that I will love you—no matter what!

READ ON YOUR OWN

Jeremiah 31:3; Isaiah 61:10; Psalm 107:8

I Won't Leave You—Ever

Be strong and courageous. Do not be afraid or terrified because of them, for the LORD your God goes with you; he will never leave you nor forsake you.
—Deuteronomy 31:6

Do not be afraid, for I am with you—always! No matter what happens, I will never abandon you. Think about that. Let that soak into your mind and heart.

If you get angry and say something that you shouldn't—I'm still with you.

If you take the easy way out and tell a lie to cover up something you did wrong—I'm still with you.

If you forget about Me and try to live life the way you want to—I'm still with you.

Sometimes the things you do will make Me happy. Sometimes the things you do will make Me sad. But there is nothing you can do that will *ever* make Me leave you.

READ ON YOUR OWN

Mark 4:39; Psalm 46:2; Psalm 73:23–24

Your Amazing Mind

*So God created man in his own image, in the image
of God he created him; male and female he created them.*
—Genesis 1:27

I created you in My own image. You are the best of My creation. I gave you a mind that is capable of amazing, creative thoughts. And I risked everything by giving you the freedom to think for yourself. Your wonderful human mind makes you totally different from animals and robots.

I could have created you so that you *had* to always love Me and seek Me. But I wanted you to use your mind to *choose* loving and seeking Me.

Your mind is amazing. It can imagine, it can dream, and it can also rebel. Bring your mind and thoughts to Me. Let Me take away the anger, the doubts, the rebellion—and give you Love, Faith, and Peace.

READ ON YOUR OWN

Genesis 1:26; Romans 8:6

Are You Listening?

My sheep listen to my voice; I know them, and they follow me.
—John 10:27

Listen to Me at all times. I have so many things to tell you. There are people and situations I want you to pray for. There is help I want to give you. There are both traps and blessings I want to point out to you. Tune out all the noise of this world, and let My Spirit help you tune in to Me.

I know you have plans for this day, but check with Me first. Your plans may fit perfectly with Mine. Or I might have something even better prepared for you. Don't get so caught up in making your day go the way you have planned, that you miss out on the blessings of *My* plan. Take time to listen to Me—and I will show you how to really live!

READ ON YOUR OWN

John 8:36; Proverbs 19:21

Pray First

You have shown me the path to life,
and you make me glad by being near to me.
—Psalm 16:11 (CEV)

Keep your eyes on Me. I will show you what I want you to do, and I will give you the strength to do it. I will never ask you to do anything without giving you what you need to do it. But you must first seek Me.

Whenever you have a decision to make, pray about it first. If you have a chance to serve Me, pray about it first. Before you begin anything, pray about it first. Seek My will in everything you do.

And when you pray, enjoy the time you spend with Me. Remember, you are in the presence of the Creator of the world, and you have My undivided attention.

READ ON YOUR OWN

Psalm 141:8

Let Me Be Your God

Be still, and know that I am God.
—Psalm 46:10

As you live your life with Me, there will be times to be busy and times to be still. I know you have many things to do. But there are times when I want you to stop everything and be still. Rest in My Presence. Listen to Me, and let Me prepare you for the day.

Sometimes when you try to be still, fears and worries creep into your mind. Then you start planning ways to avoid the things that scare you. Soon, your thoughts are far away from Me. When you feel that happening, bring your thoughts back to Me. Stop your planning. Remember that I am always with you, so there is no reason to worry or fear. Be still, and let Me be your God.

READ ON YOUR OWN

Romans 8:1

In the Right Direction

We must keep our eyes on Jesus,
who leads us and makes our faith complete.
—Hebrews 12:2 (CEV)

When you learn to ride a bike, you quickly learn to keep your eyes on where you want the bike to go. If you look away, then you're likely to go off in the wrong direction—and crash into a ditch or a tree! Wherever your eyes go, your bike soon follows.

Your thoughts are much the same. Keep your thoughts focused on Me and My will for you. People and situations change all the time. And the world whirls around like the scenery flying past a car window. If you focus too long on the world, you will get dizzy and confused. But I never change. Keep your thoughts on Me, and I will keep you moving in the right direction.

READ ON YOUR OWN

Psalm 102:27

Let Your Problems Lift You Up

So we do not give up. Our physical body is becoming older
and weaker, but our spirit inside us is made new every day.
—2 Corinthians 4:16 (ICB)

W hen a problem pops up in your life, be glad. It isn't just a problem. It's a chance to see things from My point of view.

A problem gives you two choices. You can get upset and throw a fit, which will take you down into a pit of feeling sorry for yourself. *Or* you can see the problem as a ladder, a chance to climb up into My Presence. There, in the Light of My Presence, you can see your problem as I see it—a temporary thing that will go away in time. You may even learn something from it.

This world will tell you that problems bring you down and make you weaker. But I say, problems are a chance for you to be lifted up and made stronger.

READ ON YOUR OWN

2 Corinthians 4:17–18; Psalm 89:15

Empty Hands and an Open Heart

He gives strength to the weary and increases the power of the weak.
—Isaiah 40:29

C ome to Me with empty hands and an open heart. I will fill your hands with My blessings and your heart with My Love.

I know every need that you have in your life—big and small. I know about your needs for food, clothing, and shelter. I also know your needs for friendship, for belonging, for love and acceptance. And I know that your life has been tough at times, and you get tired.

So come to Me. I will give you all you need. I will give you the strength to keep going. I will be the Friend who never lets you down. And I will love and accept you—always.

READ ON YOUR OWN

John 17:20–23; Isaiah 40:30–31

I'm Right Next to You

Because of the L<small>ORD</small>'s great love we are not consumed,
for his compassions never fail. They are new every morning;
great is your faithfulness.
—Lamentations 3:22–23

You have many choices to make today. You must decide what to wear, what to eat, and where to sit on the bus. You may also have to decide what to say to the friend who is hurting, how to handle a disappointment, and what to do about that problem at home. There are hundreds of choices to make every day. It can all be so confusing. How do you know what to choose?

Let Me help. Start by asking for My guidance. Then make one choice at a time. Don't confuse yourself by looking at all the choices at once. Instead of trying to plan the whole day, focus on My Presence with you. I'm right here next to you, and I'll help you make each choice as it comes your way.

READ ON YOUR OWN

Lamentations 3:24–26; Psalm 34:8

So Many Blessings

Therefore, since we are receiving a kingdom
that cannot be shaken, let us be thankful.
—Hebrews 12:28

L et Me teach you how to be thankful. First, think about all the things you have to be thankful for—home, family, friends, food, clothes, stuff. Then, think about how each of these things is a gift from Me.

As the sun rises, remember that today is a gift from Me. As you get out of bed, think about the gift of a healthy body. As you gather up your schoolwork and prepare for the day, be grateful for your abilities and talents. Try to count the many good things I have filled your life with. Is it twenty-five? Fifty? One hundred? I dare you to try to count all My blessings.

The secret to being thankful is thinking about all the good things in your life—and then remembering that these are all gifts from Me.

READ ON YOUR OWN

Hebrews 12:29; Psalm 119:105

Room for Me

The Lord said to me, "My grace is enough for you. When you are weak,
then my power is made perfect in you." So I am very happy to brag
about my weaknesses. Then Christ's power can live in me.
—2 Corinthians 12:9 (ICB)

When you don't have enough of something you need—time, energy, money—consider yourself blessed. Why? Because when you need something that you cannot get for yourself, you're more likely to realize what you actually need the most: *Me*. You learn to depend on Me.

This world tells you that if you depend on anyone, you are weak. But the world has it all wrong. Depending on Me doesn't make you weak. It allows Me to make you strong! Because when you feel weak and empty inside, then there is plenty of room for Me to fill you up with My Power.

READ ON YOUR OWN

James 1:2

MAY

Honor the Lᴏʀᴅ for the glory of
his name. Worship the Lᴏʀᴅ in
the splendor of his holiness.

—Psalm 29:2 (ɴʟᴛ)

Here-and-Now

God will help those who live in darkness, in the fear of death.
He will guide us into the path that goes toward peace.
—Luke 1:79 (ICB)

I have lovingly created a path for your life. Nothing is by accident. Every twist, every turn, is a part of My plan.

Don't try to see what is up ahead on your path. And don't keep turning around and looking at the past. *Here-and-Now* is the only place you can live. When you are constantly looking at the past or the future, today slips through your fingers, half-lived. Don't worry about the test you blew last week. Don't worry about whether or not you'll get invited to that party next week. Letting go of past and future worries frees you up to enjoy the Here-and-Now.

Today is the day that is filled with My glorious Presence. Today is the day I have filled with blessings. Today is the day I give you My Peace.

READ ON YOUR OWN

Luke 12:25–26

Whisper "Jesus"

Being afraid of people can get you into trouble.
But if you trust the Lord, you will be safe.
—Proverbs 29:25 (ICB)

Living to please Me is the only way to have a truly joy-filled life. Find your strength and peace in Me—not other people.

It can be fun to be part of the in-crowd. It can also be very lonely when you are left out. Sometimes you feel you would do just about anything to try to fit in. But don't let pleasing others become the only thing you think about. That can be dangerous. You can find yourself doing things you know are wrong. When you become a slave to pleasing people, you forget about Me.

If you find this happening to you, just whisper "Jesus." This simple act of trust will bring Me back to the center of your thoughts, where I belong. Concentrate on pleasing Me. And let My Light shine through you, so that others will want to enjoy My Presence—and not worry about the in-crowd.

READ ON YOUR OWN

John 10:10

May 3

Let Me Be Your Master

No one can serve two masters. Either he will hate the one and love the other, or he will be devoted to the one and despise the other.
—Matthew 6:24

It is impossible to serve two masters. You will become a slave to one and then forget the other. This means that whatever you spend your time and thoughts on becomes your master. Make sure *I* am that master. Make Me your *First Love*.

If you spend too much time and energy trying to impress your friends, then friends are your master. If all you think about is trying to beat your best score, then a game is your master. If your greatest desire is getting all A's on your report card, then grades are your master.

But friends don't always know what is best for you, games can break, and school isn't forever. Only *I* am forever. Give your heart to Me and let Me be your Master. You see, I won't make you My slave—I make you My child.

> ### READ ON YOUR OWN
> Revelation 2:4; Ephesians 3:16–17; Psalm 16:11

I Will Fill Your Life with Riches

*Give unto the L*ORD *the glory due to His name;*
*worship the L*ORD *in the beauty of holiness.*
—Psalm 29:2 (NKJV)

Worship Me, and I will fill your life with glorious riches.

The world tells you that riches are money, cars, designer clothes, and beautiful jewelry. The world says grab them and hold on tight; store up these treasures for yourself.

But My riches are the far better treasures of Joy, Love, and Peace. And instead of storing them up only for yourself, I want you to share them. When you share My riches, they multiply—so that you and those around you are richer than ever before.

How can you get My riches? Worship Me! Come to Me in the quietness of morning. Praise Me for the beauty of a new day. Sing to Me of My holiness. Open your heart to Me, and let Me flood your soul with My riches.

READ ON YOUR OWN

1 Peter 1:8

I Am Good

Let us come before him with thanksgiving
and extol him with music and song.
—Psalm 95:2

I am good. I am not just good one day and then not-so-good the next. I am *always* good. I will always do what is good and best for you.

And I am *completely* good. Not just mostly good, or 99.9 percent good. I am Light, and there is no darkness in Me—none at all!

So come to Me with a thankful heart. Be glad that your life is not at the whim of an imperfect God. Be grateful that you serve a perfect God who wants only the very best for you. Expect Me to take care of you. There is not a single thing you need that I cannot give you.

READ ON YOUR OWN

1 John 1:5

Perfect Security

So we don't look at the troubles we can see now; rather, we fix our gaze on things that cannot be seen. For the things we see now will soon be gone, but the things we cannot see will last forever.
—2 Corinthians 4:18 (NLT)

S ometimes you make checklists for yourself to help you feel in control of your life. *If I get an A, my parents will be proud of me. If I get the right clothes, then so-and-so will be my friend. If I can only . . .* The problem is that there is never an end to these lists. If you check off one thing, two or three more pop up to take its place. The harder you try to make everything just right, the more frustrated you become.

You won't find real peace and security in the things of this world, because this world is imperfect and things don't last forever. Only *I* am perfect. Only I am forever. So bring your checklist to Me. I will help you sort out what is important and what is not. Stay close to Me, and I will give you My perfect Peace.

READ ON YOUR OWN

Isaiah 26:3

Defeating Evil

*You intended to harm me, but God intended it all for good. He brought
me to this position so I could save the lives of many people.*
—Genesis 50:20 (NLT)

If you learn to trust Me—*really* trust Me—with all your heart
and soul, then nothing can separate you from My Peace. I can
use all your problems—even huge ones—to train you in trusting
Me. This is how you defeat the evil one. You let Me use the problems he throws your way to make you stronger.

Remember Joseph? His jealous brothers sold him into slavery
in Egypt. But he never stopped trusting Me. So I was able to use
that terrible thing to save not only Joseph and his family, but a
whole nation of people.

Don't be afraid of what this day—or any day—might bring. Put
your energy into trusting Me. Remind yourself that I am in complete control, and I can bring good out of any situation.

READ ON YOUR OWN

Psalm 23:4

Smile in the Face of Trouble

I can do all things through Christ who strengthens me.
—Philippians 4:13 (NKJV)

Don't waste your time wishing all your problems away. In this world, you *will* have problems. That's just the way it is here. But rejoice and be thankful! Why? Because you're My child, and that means you have an eternity of problem-free living waiting for you—in heaven. No one can take that awesome future away from you!

And while you are here on earth, I will equip you for whatever troubles come your way. Start each day by asking for My help. Tell Me everything that is worrying you, and I will guide you through your troubles. I promise.

Try to see problems as I see them—challenges that you and I can handle together. Challenges that will make you stronger. Remember, together you and I can do anything—even smile in the face of trouble.

READ ON YOUR OWN

John 16:33; Isaiah 41:13

Watch to See What I Will Do

But as for me, I watch in hope for the Lᴏʀᴅ,
I wait for God my Savior; my God will hear me.
—Micah 7:7

You are human, and that means you *will* make mistakes. So don't be so hard on yourself. And don't waste time thinking about past mistakes. That only makes you feel like a failure. Instead, bring your mistakes to Me. I can use them to make something good happen. Let Me use My creativity to weave your choices—good and bad—into something beautiful.

Try to see your mistakes as blessings that can help you be more understanding of others. For example, when you are angry and say the wrong thing to a friend, that mistake can help you understand—and forgive—someone who says something unkind to you. More importantly, mistakes give you the chance to trust Me to bring something good out of everything. Bring Me your mistakes—and then watch to see what I will do with them.

READ ON YOUR OWN

Romans 8:28

Troubles into Triumph

. . . always giving thanks to God the Father for everything,
in the name of our Lord Jesus Christ.
—Ephesians 5:20

D on't try to run away from the problems in your life. Those problems aren't just random mistakes. They are blessings in disguise. And I can use them to make your faith stronger. So instead of worrying about problems, see them as a chance to trust Me more.

When you start to feel stressed, that is a sign that you need My help. And it's okay to need My help—I *created* you to need Me. This world idolizes those who don't seem to need help from anyone. But in My kingdom I bless those who come to Me and ask for My help. As you practice trusting Me, you will see that I have the Power to turn problems into possibilities and troubles into triumphs.

So when a problem comes your way, be thankful. And let that problem lead you into a closer relationship with Me.

READ ON YOUR OWN

John 15:5; 2 Corinthians 1:8–9

Don't Borrow Worries

Peace I leave with you; my peace I give you.
—John 14:27

Whenever your mind gets stuck on a problem, bring it to Me and thank Me for it. Ask Me to show you My way of handling it. When you do this, your mind is freed and the problem is robbed of its power to make you worry. Together, we will deal with your problem, either facing it right now or putting it aside for later.

You see, many of the worries that tangle up your mind today are actually ones that you have borrowed from tomorrow. Don't waste time worrying about whether or not you will make the team next year, or pass the class next semester, or even what you will do this weekend. Give those borrowed worries to Me and let Me put them in the future where they belong. Leave them there—out of sight—and I will replace them with My Peace.

READ ON YOUR OWN

Philippians 4:6

Reach Out with *My* Love

Come to me, all you who are weary and burdened, and I will give you rest. Take my yoke upon you and learn from me, for I am gentle and humble in heart, and you will find rest for your souls.
—Matthew 11:28–29

Learn to see others through the eyes of My Love rather than your own. Your love is human and limited. It can easily get tangled up with your weaknesses and selfishness.

I want you to reach out to others with *My* Love, which is perfect and unlimited and always available. Ask Me to love others through you, and My Presence will bless not only you, but also those around you.

When you try to help others with just your *own* love, you can get all worn out. So don't forget to rest. Not just a nap or a good night's sleep, but a spiritual rest. Take time to rest in My Presence, and let Me fill you up with My Love. I will give you new energy and new strength. And I will give you rest for your soul.

READ ON YOUR OWN

Exodus 33:14

One of *My* Days

Cast all your anxiety on him because he cares for you.
—1 Peter 5:7

It has been one of those days when anything that could possibly go wrong, does go wrong. When it's been "one of those days," look for Me. Because when everything goes wrong, that is when I am working the hardest in your life. I take frustrations and turn them into opportunities to strengthen your faith. I take disappointments and turn them into chances to draw closer to Me. I take troubles and turn them into opportunities to trust Me.

Do you trust Me enough to let Me lead you through the days when everything goes wrong? Or are you determined to fix it all yourself? If you keep trying to make things go *your* way while I am leading you in a different way, you make your desires an idol. Instead of doing this, cast all your troubles and worries on Me. Then I will turn "one of those days" into one of *My* days!

READ ON YOUR OWN

1 Peter 5:6; 1 Thessalonians 5:18

I Can Use You

God can do everything!
—Luke 1:37 (ICB)

I am the mighty, all-powerful God. *Nothing* is too difficult for Me. Yet, I choose to work through you—with all your weaknesses and struggles—to carry out My plans. In fact, it is *because* you have weaknesses that you are able to receive My Power. Your struggles teach you to depend on Me.

Don't be afraid if I ask you to do something that seems too difficult. Count on Me to give you all the help you need. If I ask you to refuse to do something that is wrong, I will give you courage. If I ask you to help someone, I will give you the time and energy. If I ask you to share your faith with a friend, I will give you the words to say.

Don't try to figure things out all by yourself. Remember that I am with you, and depend on Me to help you. I can do everything—and I can use *you* to do what I ask of you.

READ ON YOUR OWN

2 Corinthians 12:9

Take Up Your Shield

In addition to all this, take up the shield of faith,
with which you can extinguish all the flaming arrows of the evil one.
—Ephesians 6:16

There is a battle going on every day—a battle for your mind. And Satan has an unlimited supply of arrows. His arrows are the lies that he whispers to you, trying to weaken your faith. His arrows say, "No one loves you," "Even Jesus wouldn't forgive that," "There's no hope for you," "You are so worthless" . . . lie after lie after lie.

Protect yourself with your shield of faith. When you feel the sting of one of Satan's lies, come to Me and hear My truth. The truth is, I love you so much that I died for you. There is nothing you can do that I won't forgive. In Me, there is always hope. And you are My own special creation, always precious to Me.

Take up your shield of faith. Stand up to the devil, and he will run away from you. Come close to Me, and I will come close to you.

READ ON YOUR OWN

James 4:7–8; Revelation 12:10

I Am Lord!

Many are the plans in a man's heart,
but it is the LORD's purpose that prevails.
—Proverbs 19:21

I am your Lord! I am the Friend who is always with you, but you must remember that I am also your Lord. I am King over all. And I want to be the King of your life.

As you begin each day, talk to Me about it. And as you go through your day, keep checking in with Me. Keep asking for My guidance. It's okay to make some plans, but be open to changes in those plans. I may have other ideas for your day.

Don't try to skip ahead or take shortcuts. Concentrate on the task that is right before you. Do your very best at that. Then trust Me to show you what to do next. I will guide you step by step, leading you along a path of peace.

READ ON YOUR OWN

Luke 1:79

I Never Run Out

*And my God will meet all your needs according
to his glorious riches in Christ Jesus.*
—Philippians 4:19

I am a God of plenty. I never run out of good things.

I never run out of Love. I never run out of Peace. I never run out of forgiveness or mercy. I never run out of time to listen to you. I never run out of blessings to give you.

You live in a world where there often isn't enough, where even food and water are sometimes scarce. Even if you have enough yourself, you know there are many places around the world where children are hungry. So I understand that it may be difficult for you to believe I never run out.

Hunger and poverty are problems of this world. And I want you to be My hands to help those around you who are in need. But while you are reaching out to others, reach out to Me for My blessings—which never run out.

READ ON YOUR OWN

2 Corinthians 5:7

Puzzle Pieces

For as the heavens are higher than the earth, so are My ways higher than your ways, and My thoughts than your thoughts.
—Isaiah 55:9 (NKJV)

I gave you an amazing mind. With it you can think great thoughts and dream great dreams. But My Mind is infinitely bigger and more amazing. My thoughts contain all of creation and the universe, all of the past, present, and future. And because I understand all things and all times, My thoughts and My ways are different from yours.

Life can be like a box of puzzle pieces—with the box top missing. When you look around at your life, all you can see are the pieces. But I see the final picture. I know how all the pieces fit together. I know how to join together all the jagged pieces of hurts and disappointments, plus the smooth pieces of victories and joys.

Trust My timing and My ways. Trust Me to fit all your pieces together into a wonderful life. And trust Me—at the end of your life—to lead you home to heaven.

READ ON YOUR OWN

Isaiah 55:8; Psalm 73:23–24

You Are Safe with Me

The LORD gives strength to his people;
the LORD blesses his people with peace.
—Psalm 29:11

You are completely safe and secure in My Presence—even when you don't feel that way. You are never separated from Me because I never leave you.

When you forget that I am with you, you may feel lonely or afraid. If that happens, say a prayer or whisper My Name: "Jesus." This will remind you that I am still right beside you. As you focus on Me, I will replace your loneliness and fear with My Peace.

As wonderful as My Peace is now, it is nothing compared to heaven. In heaven I will still be right by your side, but you will be able to *see* Me. You and I will talk face-to-Face. And your Joy will be bigger and better than anything you can imagine!

READ ON YOUR OWN

1 Corinthians 13:12

Live in My Light

But if we live in the light, as God does, we share in life with each other.
And the blood of his Son Jesus washes all our sins away.
—1 John 1:7 (CEV)

When you carry around sins, it is like carrying a backpack filled with rocks. The rocks are called *shame*, *guilt*, *self-pity*, *jealousy*, and even *hatred*. As time goes on, your pack gets heavier and heavier, pulling you down.

Give it to Me, all of it. Tell me your sins and hand over that backpack. I want to dump out all the heavy rocks. Then I want to fill your backpack up again with *love*, *mercy*, *forgiveness, joy*, and *peace*. Instead of weighing you down, these things will lift you up and make your journey easier.

Don't be embarrassed to bring your sins to Me. I already know all about them, and I'm just waiting to forgive you. That is why I died on the cross—to take the punishment for your sins. Don't live in the darkness of sin. Live in the Light of My forgiveness.

READ ON YOUR OWN

Isaiah 61:10; John 8:12

What More Could You Need?

He who did not spare his own Son, but gave him up for us all—how will he not also, along with him, graciously give us all things?
—Romans 8:32

I, the Creator of the whole universe, am with you and for you. What more could you need? So there is no need to worry about anything—ever.

And yet, you do worry. The funny thing about worry is that it takes up a lot of time, but it doesn't really accomplish anything. Worrying about a sin won't make it go away; asking My forgiveness will. Worrying about a problem at home or at school won't do any good; praying about it will. Worrying about what to say to a hurting friend won't help; asking for My help will.

Worry happens when you try to snatch back control of your life from Me. You forget that I am in charge. The only cure is to stop thinking about your problem and start thinking about Me. Let Me have control. After all, I gave up My Life for you. How could I not give you everything else you need?

READ ON YOUR OWN

Romans 8:31; Micah 7:7

Don't Get Stuck

Jesus answered, "I am the way and the truth and the life.
No one comes to the Father except through me."
—John 14:6

I am the Way, the Truth, and the Life. But sometimes it can be hard for you to understand My way of doing things in this life. It's easy to get your mind stuck on your own idea of how things should go. Just don't get so stuck on your idea that you forget to look for My way.

When things are not going your way, don't panic—accept the situation. Feeling sorry for yourself can easily spill over into feelings of resentment and anger. That can cause you to push away from Me.

Remember that I use all things to work together for good in your life—even the things you wish were different. So accept your situation, and then look around you for what I am doing. Keep your eyes on Me—no matter what is happening around you. When you keep Me in the center of your thinking, I help you make good choices.

READ ON YOUR OWN

1 Peter 5:6; Romans 8:28

May 23

Hidden Treasures

The Lord will be your safety. He is full of salvation, wisdom and knowledge. Respect for the Lord is the greatest treasure.
—Isaiah 33:6 (ICB)

B efore you even get out of bed in the morning, I have already looked ahead at your day and prepared the path that will get you through this day. And it's not just an empty, boring path. It's loaded with treasures I've hidden all along the way. Some treasures are blessings—sunshine, flowers, birds, friendships, answered prayers. Other treasures are troubles—designed to shake you free from old habits and help you see things in a new way.

But *all* of My treasures are to help you remember that I am always with you. So as you go through this day, look for signs of Me all around you. You will find Me all along the way.

READ ON YOUR OWN

Colossians 2:2–3

The Fifth Dimension

Blessed are those who have learned to acclaim you,
who walk in the light of your presence, O Lord.
—Psalm 89:15

You've heard of 3-D. Some movies use 3-D technology to adjust the three dimensions (length, width, and height) of an image—to make you feel as if you're actually part of the action. There is also a fourth dimension: time. These four dimensions work together to pinpoint the place and time of your life on this earth. But I want you to consider a fifth dimension—My Presence in your life.

I control the three dimensions of space and the one of time. That is how I am able to be *all* places at *all* times. And that is how I can know everything you will need—to get through this day, and the next, and the next.

Open your heart to the fifth dimension—the most exciting one of all: My Presence with you.

READ ON YOUR OWN

Genesis 3:8

Untangling the Knots

A righteous man may have many troubles,
*but the L*ORD *delivers him from them all.*
—Psalm 34:19

T he world can feel overwhelming. Sometimes your mind
jumps from problem to problem to problem—until your
thoughts get all tangled up in knots. You can't think clearly, you
forget about Me, and your mind becomes dark with worry.

I want to rush in and straighten everything out for you. I want
to take away all your worries. But I won't—unless you ask Me.
I gave you the freedom to choose; I won't force you to take My
help. I will wait for you to remember Me and ask Me to help you.

Just call My Name. Give Me your problems and your worry-
thoughts. I'll untangle all the knots, and together we will handle
whatever this day brings.

READ ON YOUR OWN

Isaiah 41:10; Zephaniah 3:17

Exactly the Same

*I am the Alpha and the Omega, the First and the Last,
the Beginning and the End.*
—Revelation 22:13

In a world where everything changes—the weather, your friends, and sometimes even your family—I am the One who never changes. I am exactly the same as I was at the beginning of the world, and I will be exactly the same at the end of it. You can always count on Me.

I created a beautiful, perfect world for you. But sin came into the world, and since then the world is constantly changing. Nothing stays the same, and nothing is ever for certain—in this world. But remember that I have overcome the world. So stay close to Me. In My never-changing, always-loving Presence, you can face the changes of this world with peace—*My* Peace.

READ ON YOUR OWN

John 16:33

Put Me On

Clothe yourselves with the Lord Jesus Christ.
—Romans 13:14

Every morning you put on the clothes you need for that day. A jacket for cooler days. Boots for rain. Sweats for exercising. Putting on the right clothes prepares you for your day.

Clothes take care of the outside, but what about the inside? I have a suggestion: Put *Me* on. Wear *Me*. This will prepare you for your day.

How? "Put Me on" by talking to Me first thing in the morning. And then "wear Me" throughout the day by keeping Me in your thoughts. Keep checking in, because things change. Just as a change in the weather might call for a change in clothes, a change in your world might call for a change from Me. Maybe this morning you needed encouragement, but now a little forgiveness is what you need.

So clothe yourself with Me—it's the best way to start your day.

READ ON YOUR OWN

Psalm 27:8; Colossians 3:12

See My Greatness

Great is the LORD and most worthy of praise;
his greatness no one can fathom.
—Psalm 145:3

Let Me surround you with My Presence. I am King of kings and Lord of lords. When you come close to Me, I come even closer to you. You may feel overwhelmed by My Power and Glory. You may feel small compared to My Greatness. These feelings are actually a form of worship. You are telling Me that you know how powerful and wonderful I am.

Some people do not like My Greatness. They don't like feeling small compared to *anything*—not even Me. They want to be in complete control, and they want to be the most important. They may even be so wrapped up in themselves that they don't see Me at all.

Don't fall into that trap. Enjoy being in the presence of My Greatness. Be glad that you have such a great and all-powerful God who loves you and is taking care of you.

READ ON YOUR OWN

1 Timothy 6:15–16; James 4:8; Acts 17:28; Psalm 145:4–6

Just What You Need

"They will call him Immanuel"—which means, "God with us."
—Matthew 1:23

I am Immanuel. My Name means *God with you*. And that is who I am. I am God, and I am always with you, constantly watching over you. You are surrounded by My Love and My Presence. There is nothing that can ever separate you from Me—not even the worst of troubles.

Some people feel closest to Me during happy times, when they can see My blessings and sing My praises. Others feel closest to Me in times of trouble—when their trust in Me helps them feel My hand leading them to safety. But both the troubles and the joys are My gifts to you.

Each day I provide just what you need, to draw you closer to Me. Try to see everything that happens as My gift designed just for you. This helps you to be thankful—even in times of trouble.

READ ON YOUR OWN

Colossians 2:6–7

The Gift of Your Time

For the eyes of the Lord range throughout the earth to strengthen those whose hearts are fully committed to him.
—2 Chronicles 16:9

Don't rush through our time together. When you are in a hurry, your mind flips back and forth between Me and the things you are about to do. You have My full attention; I want your full attention too.

Set aside a special time every day just to be with Me. It can be early in the morning or just before you go to sleep. It can be soon after you get home from school. But don't let other things crowd out our time together. Then look for a quiet place where you can relax in My Presence. Perhaps it's a cozy spot in the den, or in your room. Or maybe it's outside under a tree. Find a peaceful place for us to meet. Look forward to our time together!

When you bring Me the gift of your time, I strengthen you and prepare you for what is ahead of you—this day and all your days.

READ ON YOUR OWN

Psalm 119:27; Hebrews 13:15

Let Me Stop the Storm

Now may the Lord of peace himself give you peace
at all times and in every way.
—2 Thessalonians 3:16

You have heard people talk about having a *brainstorm*. They mean that someone has just had a very good idea. But I have another definition. A *brainstorm* is when you put all of your mental energy into trying to figure things out for yourself. Thoughts are spinning round and round, but going nowhere and accomplishing nothing. It's as if they are caught up in a terrible storm. All the while, My Peace hovers over you, searching for a place to land.

Let Me stop the storm in your mind. Be still, and ask Me to take control of your thoughts. Just as I calmed the winds and waves for My disciples, I will calm the storm of thoughts inside your brain. Ask Me for My Peace—it's there whenever you need it.

READ ON YOUR OWN

Matthew 8:23-26; Job 22:21

JUNE

I am the LORD your God. I am
holding your hand, so don't be
afraid. I am here to help you.

—Isaiah 41:13 (CEV)

Don't Look
for Unnecessary Trouble

As for God, his way is perfect; the word of the Lord is flawless.
—Psalm 18:30

I am involved in each moment of your life. I have carefully mapped out every inch of your journey through this day. But because there is sin in the world, things will sometimes get messy. There will be trouble. But trust that I have already planned a perfect way for you to get through your problems.

And while you must face some trouble, don't add to your problems by forgetting to let Me guide you. I will lead you *around* some of the trouble that you see up ahead. Remember that I am with you every second. Let the Light of My Presence show you the way to go—giving you Peace and Joy that trouble can't take away from you.

READ ON YOUR OWN

Isaiah 41:13

You Are My Child

Now we are children of God.
—1 John 3:2

I am God, and you are My child. And like so many parents on earth, I want you to grow up to be like Me. To become more like Me, you need to spend time with Me. Relax in My Presence, while I work in your heart and mind. Let go of cares and worries so that you can receive My Peace. *Be still, and know that I am God.*

Don't worry about what others think. Don't worry about what's "cool" or "in." And don't be like the Pharisees in the Bible. They got so wrapped up in their own rules that they lost sight of Me.

Keep your eyes on Me, and remember how much I love you. This helps you love Me and also love others with *My* Love.

READ ON YOUR OWN

Psalm 46:10

When You Are Afraid . . .

Where God's love is, there is no fear,
because God's perfect love takes away fear.
—1 John 4:18 (ICB)

I want to be the Center of your life. When you focus on Me, My Peace chases away your fears and worries.

I know . . . *everyone* is afraid sometimes. I am not saying that you will *never* be afraid. What I am saying is that you never have to face your fears alone. I am *always* with you, and My Strength is *always* there for you. I will *never* leave you.

But fear is a sneaky thing. Just when you think you've gotten it out of your life, it will creep up behind and whisper in your ear: *You're all alone.* But remember My words: *I am always with you.*

Thank Me for My Presence, and trust Me; this will protect you from fear. Spend time in the Light of My Love, while I bless you with My Peace.

READ ON YOUR OWN

2 Thessalonians 3:16

Worth Celebrating

Consider it pure joy, my brothers,
whenever you face trials of many kinds.
—James 1:2

Consider problems as pure joy. That's not the way the world usually looks at problems, is it? The world says to do everything you can to *avoid* problems. But there is simply no way to avoid every problem, no matter how hard you try.

The best way to get through a difficult day is to hold My hand tightly and keep talking to Me. As we talk, be sure to tell Me you trust Me—and thank Me for My help. Ask Me to guide you through your problems and show you the blessings hidden in them.

The blessing of self-control can be learned from dealing with a difficult teacher. The blessing of patience can be learned from an illness. I teach you many things through your problems. I also use them to draw you closer to Me.

So yes, consider problems as pure joy, knowing that with Me by your side, they can become things worth celebrating.

READ ON YOUR OWN

Philippians 4:13; Isaiah 26:3

Seeking Perfection

You shall have no other gods before me.
—Exodus 20:3

I created every person—including you—with a longing for perfection. Most people try to fill this longing with things from this world. They try to have the coolest stuff and the latest fashions. They try to be the most popular in their class, or the star of the sports field or the stage. Some even try drugs or alcohol.

Some people will do anything and everything to fill that longing, except turn to Me. Whatever you desire the most—whatever you worship with your time and attention—becomes your god, your idol. But you must have no other gods before Me! Only *I* am God. Only *I* am worthy of your worship and praise. And only *I* can fill your longing for perfection.

READ ON YOUR OWN

Psalm 37:4

You Will Find Me

The heavens declare the glory of God;
the skies proclaim the work of his hands.
—Psalm 19:1

The beauty of creation is a sign—pointing straight to Me.

The vastness of the heavens declares the vastness of My Being. The rock-solid mountains tell you that I am a God who is rock-solid and does not change. The quiet peace and mysteries of space are a hint of My Peace, which is without end and beyond understanding. The thousand details of even the tiniest wildflower are to help you remember that I know every detail of your life. And the depths of the ocean are to remind you of the depths of My Love.

Creation declares My Glory to anyone who is willing to see. So open your eyes. See that I am Lord of all creation! Seek My Face in the beauty of the world around you. And I promise you will find Me.

READ ON YOUR OWN

Psalm 105:4; Psalm 19:2; Isaiah 60:2

I Am Enough!

But seek his kingdom, and these things will be given to you as well.
—Luke 12:31

I am all around you. Even when you don't notice Me, I am here.

You may not notice Me because your mind is tied up with other things. Like worry. A lot of people believe that worry is just a part of life. But they are wrong. Worry is actually a kind of unbelief. Worrying says you don't believe I am big enough to take care of whatever it is that upsets you so much. Worrying says you think I need *your* help.

Wrong! I am big enough. I am strong enough. I love you enough. Bring your problems to Me. You can trust Me to take care of you—*and* whatever you are worrying about!

READ ON YOUR OWN

Luke 12:22–30; John 16:33

I Did It All for You

*Then Jesus came to them and said, "All authority
in heaven and on earth has been given to me."*
—Matthew 28:18

I am all-powerful. All of heaven and earth is at My command.
And yet . . .

I gave up all the glory and perfection of heaven to come to earth
as a baby—for you. I grew up here, in the dust and sin of this
world—for you. I allowed Myself to be beaten and then cruelly
killed on a cross—for you. I rose from the grave and defeated
death and the devil—for you. I did it *all* for you, so that you could
be forgiven of your sins and live forever with Me.

I gave everything for you. Don't hold back anything from Me.
Bring Me your secret thoughts, your problems, and most of all,
your heart. Come to Me with a thankful heart—ready to learn
and be changed.

READ ON YOUR OWN

Psalm 100:4

June 9

Love Takes Care of It All

Above all, love each other deeply,
because love covers over a multitude of sins.
—1 Peter 4:8

Love is the key to My kingdom. Above all else, I want you to love Me with all your heart, mind, body, and soul. When that happens, you open yourself up to receive My Love for you. And My Love changes everything.

My Love *covers over a multitude of sins*—both your sins and the sins of others. This means that once you bring your sins to Me, they are forgiven and completely forgotten. It also means that you will be able to forgive others, because you will see them through the eyes of My Love. You'll be able to look beyond a bully's hateful words, for example, and see someone who feels bad about himself. When someone lies, you will see more than just the lies: You'll see a person who is afraid to tell the truth.

Choose to see others through the eyes of My Love. And My Love will take care of it all.

READ ON YOUR OWN

1 John 4:18; Revelation 2:4

Take a Break with Me

Find rest, O my soul, in God alone; my hope comes from him.
—Psalm 62:5

Take a break. Put aside your to-do list. For a little while, put aside your chores, your practices, your playing, and even your homework. Stop trying to figure everything out, and hang out with Me. I created you to need rest. Not just the kind of rest that comes from sleeping, but the kind that comes only from spending time with Me—rest for your soul.

Ask Me to take charge of the details of your life. Remember that you are on a journey with Me. When you try to look into the future and plan for everything that might happen, you ignore your Friend who is with you all the time. While you're worrying about what's up ahead, you don't even feel the strong grip of My hand holding yours. How foolish that is, My child!

Never lose sight of My Presence with you. This will keep you resting in Me every day.

READ ON YOUR OWN

1 Thessalonians 5:17

June 11

Never Alone

If a person's thinking is controlled by his sinful self,
then there is death. But if his thinking is controlled by the Spirit,
then there is life and peace.
—Romans 8:6 (ICB)

There is a battle being fought for the control of your mind. The devil is using every weapon he can think of to win. He'll distract you—with fun, with busyness, and with noise. He'll plague you with fears, worries, and guilt over past mistakes. He'll do whatever it takes to keep your thoughts centered on yourself and away from Me.

But you are not alone in this battle. I am on your side, and I will fight with you. Your job is to call on My Spirit for help. Ask My Spirit to take control of your mind and keep your thoughts focused on Me. Then I will strengthen you so that you can withstand the devil's attacks. And I will fill your mind with Peace.

READ ON YOUR OWN

Isaiah 12:2

A Day that Is Just Right

And do not complain as some of them did.
—1 Corinthians 10:10 (ICB)

When you get up in the morning, you get to decide what kind of day you will have. I don't mean that you can decide you are going to have a completely problem-free day, a Saturday, or even a snow day. I mean that you choose how you will view this day. And there are really only two choices: to complain about everything you don't like, or to stay close to Me—so you can see things *My* way.

You can choose to see the rain, or the rainbow. You can choose to see a mountain of homework, or the chance to learn something new. You can resent your parents for not letting you go to that movie, or you can be grateful that someone cares enough to say no sometimes.

You can choose to see everything that is wrong, or you can choose to see Me. If you choose Me, I'll show you how all those wrongs can turn into a day that is just right.

READ ON YOUR OWN

Luke 1:79

June 13

Bubbling Joy

Only God's Spirit gives new life. The Spirit is like the wind that blows
wherever it wants to. You can hear the wind, but you don't know where
it comes from or where it is going.
—John 3:8 (CEV)

I am creating something new in you—a bubbling spring of Joy that splashes into others' lives. It isn't just an ordinary, temporary kind of joy, like a gift on your birthday. And it doesn't depend on what is happening around you. This is *My* Joy, and it comes from the Holy Spirit living inside you. My Joy bubbles up like the fizz of a soda, until it spills over and blesses all those around you.

Don't try to control the ways My Spirit moves through you. Just stay open, as if you were a window on a summer day.

My Spirit is like the wind. You can't see the wind, but you know it is there because you see the leaves and grass moving. In the same way, you can't see the Spirit. But you—and all those around you—can know that My Spirit is within you by the Peace, Love, and Joy that flow out of you.

READ ON YOUR OWN

Galatians 5:22

You Are My Chosen One

But you are not like that, for you are a chosen people.
You are royal priests, a holy nation, God's very own possession.
As a result, you can show others the goodness of God.
—1 Peter 2:9 (NLT)

I have always loved you—*always*. Before you were born, I knew you and I loved you. In your mother's tummy, I knew you and loved you. From the moment you were born, I knew you and loved you. And I have been right here with you every moment since then, knowing everything about you and loving you—mistakes and all.

I will never leave you or stop loving you. You are My chosen one—wearing clothes of salvation and wrapped up in My Love. I will sing to you, and I will teach you how to sing with Me. And together we will tell others about My Love, which never ends.

READ ON YOUR OWN

Jeremiah 31:3; Isaiah 61:10

June 15

Eyes to See and Ears to Hear

I wait for the Lᴏʀᴅ, my soul waits, and in his word I put my hope.
—Psalm 130:5

E *yes that see and ears that hear*—that's a phrase you find a lot in the Bible. But what does it mean? Can't everyone with eyes and ears see and hear My message? Well . . . no. Because I am found in the quiet and stillness by those who are willing to look and listen for Me.

The noise, the distractions, the busyness of this world make it difficult to recognize Me sometimes. And the devil also likes to do all that he can to keep people away from Me.

In order to see and hear Me, you have to seek Me—and wait for Me. Block out the noise of the world, and be still. Spend time alone with your Bible, or in prayer, or just listening. It is then that your eyes will see and your ears will hear My message of Hope.

READ ON YOUR OWN

2 Corinthians 4:18; Isaiah 6:3

Your Special Path

The Lord has told you what is good. He has told you what he wants
from you: Do what is right to other people. Love being kind to others.
And live humbly, trusting your God.
—Micah 6:8 (ICB)

E ven before the beginning of the world, I designed a path for you to follow. It is made just for you. In fact, I designed a path for each of My children. And each path is different. It is perfectly made for the person who will be walking it. Each path has its own high points and low points, twists and turns. Your job is to let Me lead you down your special path.

Don't let anyone tell you that his path is the only right way. And be careful not to tell anyone that only your path is the right way. Just walk closely with Me along your path, enjoying My Presence and My Peace.

As we walk down this path together, I ask three things of you: Try to do what is right, love kindness, and humbly trust in Me—wherever I lead you.

READ ON YOUR OWN

Ephesians 2:10

Laughing at Troubles

She is clothed with strength and dignity;
she can laugh at the days to come.
—Proverbs 31:25

Learn to laugh at yourself and at the world. Instead of getting bogged down in the mud of worry and fear, laugh and be happy because I am by your side. Just as parents delight in the laughter of their children, so I delight in hearing you laugh. I feel happy when you trust Me enough to enjoy your life.

Don't let worrying over troubles—especially things that haven't even happened yet—keep you from laughing. Live each day to its fullest by being full of My Joy. That doesn't mean you won't ever have any problems. It doesn't mean you won't ever be sad. But it *does* mean that when troubles come, you can still have Joy because the Creator of the universe is right there beside you— helping you with your problems.

So learn to laugh at your troubles . . . and you'll find that they aren't nearly so troublesome.

READ ON YOUR OWN

Proverbs 17:22; Matthew 1:23; Matthew 11:28–30

A Perfect Plan

In his heart a man plans his course,
*but the L*ORD *determines his steps.*
—Proverbs 16:9

I have a plan for your life, a perfect plan. But I will show you only a piece of it at a time. If I showed you the whole plan, it might overwhelm you—or you might decide to run off ahead of Me. It would be like learning that you're going to grow up to be a teacher, so today you decide to take over the class. That wouldn't work at all!

Sometimes I will give you a glimpse of your wonderful future, to encourage you to keep going. But I want you to focus on staying close to Me *today*. We will travel toward your future together, step by step. I will decide how fast or how slow we go, according to your needs. After all, you can't be a brain surgeon before you pass basic biology!

So don't crane your neck, trying to see what's around the next corner. Trust Me enough to relax and enjoy your walk with Me today.

READ ON YOUR OWN

Ephesians 1:4; Jeremiah 29:11; Ephesians 1:13–14

Shout for Joy!

But let all who take refuge in you be glad; let them ever sing for joy.
—Psalm 5:11

S ing! Dance! Shout for joy because I am your God! There is no greater reason to celebrate.

Sing of My Love and forgiveness wherever you go. Dance and shout for joy because you serve a God who loves and treasures you.

Live your life in praise to Me. Let the words you speak and the things you do bring Me Glory. I am with you always, so don't let fear silence your praise. Keep your eyes on Me, and I will keep you going in the right direction. So sing, dance, and shout for joy!

READ ON YOUR OWN

Ephesians 3:20–21; Jude 24–25; Joshua 1:5

You Can Find Me

When I consider your heavens, the work of your fingers, the moon and the stars, which you have set in place, what is man that you are mindful of him, the son of man that you care for him?
—Psalm 8:3–4

I am constantly speaking to you. But I don't always use words. Day after day, I paint amazing sunsets across the sky to show you My Power and Glory. I stroke your cheek with a gentle breeze to remind you that I am right beside you. I speak in the faces and voices of your loved ones.

You can find Me in every minute of the day, if you have eyes that are looking and ears that are listening. Ask My Spirit to help you see and hear Me better. Practice looking and listening for Me in the world around you, and gradually you will see and hear Me more. Search for Me with all your heart—and you will find Me.

READ ON YOUR OWN
Psalm 8:1–2; Psalm 19:1–2;
1 Corinthians 6:19; Jeremiah 29:13

I Am Timeless

*"I am the Alpha and the Omega," says the Lord God,
"who is, and who was, and who is to come, the Almighty."*
—Revelation 1:8

My idea of time is very different from yours, because I am timeless—beyond time. *I am. I was. And I will always be.*

Time is a protection for you. One twenty-four–hour day of life is enough for you to handle. But time can also become your master—making you its slave—if you think about it too much.

Wait with Me while I bless you. Don't think about where you have to be an hour from now. Don't worry about what you need to get done. Take off your watch and just sit with Me. As you focus on being with Me, enjoying My Presence, time will become less and less important. And I will become more and more important to you.

READ ON YOUR OWN

Micah 7:7; Numbers 6:24–26

Your Best Protection

The Lord is near.
—Philippians 4:5

I am always near. So I know that sometimes you get angry at Me—and may even feel like shaking your fist in My Face. You are tempted to complain about the way I am treating you. You want to rebel against Me. But that is a dangerous thing to do. Once you step over that line, rivers of rage and self-pity can sweep you away.

Your best protection is to thank Me for the things that are troubling you. You see, it is impossible for you to thank Me and complain at the same time. It may feel weird at first to thank Me when you are upset with Me. But keep trying. Your thankful words, prayed in faith, will change your heart and bring you closer to Me.

READ ON YOUR OWN
Psalm 116:17; Philippians 4:4, 6

June 23

Waiting to Help

Don't make God's Spirit sad. The Spirit makes you sure
that someday you will be free from your sins.
—Ephesians 4:30 (CEV)

When you choose *not* to trust Me, it hurts My heart and I grieve.

It hurts Me to see you struggle alone with problems, when I am just waiting to help you. It saddens Me to see you blindly walking through your day, not even noticing the blessings I have provided for you. And it grieves Me to see you ignore My loving Presence all around you.

But when you walk through your day trusting Me, I am overjoyed! I don't expect your walk with Me to be perfect. I know that there will be times when your thoughts wander away from Me. But when you realize this has happened, just pull your thoughts back to Me. I'll always be waiting.

READ ON YOUR OWN

Psalm 52:8; Deuteronomy 31:6

Hold My Hand

He alone is my rock and my salvation;
he is my fortress, I will not be shaken.
—Psalm 62:6

Hold My hand—and trust Me. Remember that I am always with you, taking care of you. When you are walking by My side, I will not let you fall.

I created you to enjoy being in My Presence more than anyone else's—more than friends, and even more than family. I am the only One who can satisfy those longings deep in your heart.

Worries and fears melt away in the Light of My Presence. But when you turn away from Me, you can get hurt by the darkness that is in the world. Don't be surprised by how easily you slip into sin when you forget to hold on to My hand.

In this world, depending on someone else is seen as childish and immature. But in My kingdom, the spiritual "grown-ups" are the ones who know that they always need Me.

READ ON YOUR OWN

Isaiah 41:10; Psalm 62:5

You Make Me Sing!

He will rejoice over you with singing.
—Zephaniah 3:17

When you make a special gift for someone, you can't wait to see that person open it. That smile, that hug, those words of thanks just feel so good!

I am the same way. I want you to begin each day by opening up your hands and your heart to receive My gifts. From the morning sunrise to the evening stars, I have prepared so many gifts for you. And I can't wait to see what you think of each one. Will you notice that flower I planted along your path? Will you see that cloud I shaped for you? Will you remember to thank Me?

When you praise Me for the gifts I have made, you open up your heart to Me. Your smiles, your songs, your words of praise just feel so good! Remember that I take great joy in you—you make Me sing!

READ ON YOUR OWN

Psalm 118:24; Psalm 95:2

Nothing Surprises Me

Yea, though I walk through the valley of the shadow of death,
I will fear no evil; for You are with me.
—Psalm 23:4 (NKJV)

I go before you as well as with you into this day. Nothing surprises Me. I know exactly what will happen—both the good and the bad. Trust in Me and don't be afraid. Stay close to Me, and I will not let you be overwhelmed by anything that happens today. I will help you through it all—fights with a friend, disappointments, a bad grade, temptations to sin, illness—whatever comes your way.

Don't go through today with fear in your heart because of what might or might not happen. I will help you deal with *whatever* happens—moment by moment. Facing your problems with Me brings blessings that are much bigger than your troubles. So bring all your problems to Me, and I will bless you with My Joy.

READ ON YOUR OWN

Psalm 23:1–3; 2 Corinthians 4:16–17

For Your Protection

Show me the way I should go, for to you I lift up my soul.
—Psalm 143:8

Some days are long and tough. So stop and rest with Me for a while. Don't worry about what's ahead. Don't think about the past or the future. Just focus on right here and right now—with Me.

I created time to protect you. Because I am timeless, I can see your entire life from beginning to end—all at the same time. But I knew that you couldn't bear to see your whole life all at once. So I created time to hide your future from you, to protect you.

You can do nothing about the past, so just let it go. You cannot know the future, so put it aside. Meet me here and now—in this moment of time. Trust that I am with you, watching over you wherever you go.

READ ON YOUR OWN

Genesis 28:15

I Am Good

Examine and see how good the Lord is.
Happy is the person who trusts the Lord.
—Psalm 34:8 (ICB)

I *am* good. Walk with Me today and see that for yourself. The more time you spend with Me, the more you will see just how good I am. And I promise to do only what is good for you.

When hard times come, many people start to doubt My goodness. But troubles are just part of living in this imperfect world. And I can use your troubles to grow your faith.

I know that doesn't always make sense to you. You won't always understand the "why" of things. I am God, and My thoughts and My ways are incredibly bigger and more complicated than yours. When you don't understand, just *trust* that I am good—and that I *always* work for good in your life.

READ ON YOUR OWN

Isaiah 55:8–9

Together Forever

O God, You are my God; early will I seek You.
—Psalm 63:1 (NKJV)

When you first wake up in the morning, think of Me. Remember My promise to be with you always. In fact, I have been watching over you all night long. I know it is hard to think clearly first thing in the morning; your mind is still half-asleep. But I am wide-awake and waiting for you.

Those first few thoughts in the morning can be anxious ones. *Did you finish your homework? Are you ready for the test? Are you ready to face your parents, that teacher, that bully at school? What if this happens? Or that*?

Don't start your day with all those questions. They only make you more anxious and worried. Start with *Me*. Whisper My Name and invite Me into your thoughts. Suddenly your day will be brighter as you realize you don't have to face it alone. We will deal with things *together*. This you-and-I-together promise helps you face the day cheerfully—with confidence.

READ ON YOUR OWN

Psalm 5:3; Philippians 4:13

I Know the Way

Then you will know the truth, and the truth will set you free.
—John 8:32

I am the Truth—the One who came to set you free. As you learn to let My Spirit control your mind and actions, you become free in Me—you become more and more the one I created you to be.

I do my best work in you when you sit quietly in My Presence, focusing your thoughts on Me. Open yourself to Me, letting My thoughts flow freely into your mind. I will help you see things as I see them. And I will lead you along paths of adventure.

Don't worry about what is on the road up ahead. I know the way for your life, because I *am* the Way and the Truth and the Life. Trust that you are safe with Me—the One who died to set you free.

READ ON YOUR OWN

Philippians 2:13; John 14:6

JULY

So now, those who are in
Christ Jesus are not judged guilty.

—Romans 8:1 (ICB)

Fight for Your Time with Me

God, we come into your Temple. There we think about your love.
—Psalm 48:9 (ICB)

I am Life and Light. Soak in My Presence as you would soak in a warm bathtub. Let My Love surround you and seep into your soul—giving you new energy. And let all your worries swirl away.

You need to spend time alone with Me—so I can get the tangles out of your thoughts and smooth out the day for you. Sometimes you will have to fight for this time with Me. You'll have to fight your own wish to stay in bed "just a few more minutes." You'll have to say "not right now" to friends. And you'll have to ignore the world when it says you're just sitting there, wasting time.

Fight for our time together. Find your joy in Me. I am the One your heart is looking for.

READ ON YOUR OWN

Deuteronomy 33:12; Psalm 37:4

I Am the Great Artist

*Lord, every morning you hear my voice. Every morning,
I tell you what I need. And I wait for your answer.*
—Psalm 5:3 (ICB)

Let Me show you My way for you today. Pray about everything—
the big things and the little things. Give your entire day to Me
and then wait to see what I will create with it.

I am the Great Artist, and your day is My empty canvas. Watch Me
do my work; I will paint My colors into your life—colors of My Love,
Mercy, Peace, Hope, and Joy. And you will not be disappointed.

Trust Me to take your ordinary day and create a masterpiece.

READ ON YOUR OWN

Psalm 5:2; Deuteronomy 33:27

Not Guilty

Do not judge, and you will not be judged. Do not condemn, and you will not be condemned. Forgive, and you will be forgiven.
—Luke 6:37

My children make a hobby out of judging one another—and themselves. But *I* am the only true Judge. I hate seeing My children put themselves down or judge others. This is not My way for you.

I gave you the ability to choose what is right. If you live close to Me and follow My teaching, the Spirit will guide you and correct you. I died on the cross so that you would be washed clean of all your sins. I gave My own blood so that you would be fully forgiven.

So forgive others, and forgive yourself. Let My Spirit help you make good choices and correct you when you need it. And always remember, I do not condemn My children.

READ ON YOUR OWN

2 Timothy 4:8; Titus 3:5; Romans 8:1

Singing with the Angels

God is spirit, and his worshipers must worship in spirit and in truth.
—John 4:24

Y ou've heard people say things like, "She sings like an angel." But did you know that you really can sing *with* the angels? When you worship Me in spirit and truth, your voice joins with choirs of angels who are always praising Me. While you can't hear their voices, I hear every word of your worship and praise.

To worship in spirit and in truth means that you truly *worship* Me. You don't just go through the motions—sitting and standing at the right times, closing your eyes to pray. It means that your heart and your spirit are really praising Me, because you know I am the All-Powerful God.

When you truly worship Me, it opens the way to My Heart. Then My blessings rain down on you. And the greatest blessing of all is simply being *near Me*.

READ ON YOUR OWN

John 4:23; Psalm 100:4

Jump In with Both Feet

Look at the new thing I am going to do. It is already happening.
Don't you see it? I will make a road in the desert.
I will make rivers in the dry land.
—Isaiah 43:19 (ICB)

You will never be in complete control of your life. It just isn't possible. You want to feel completely safe and secure. But even if you plan out every detail, the world will mess up your plans.

So just stop trying to be in control. Stop trying to make your life completely safe and predictable—*and boring*! Instead, grab My hand and jump in with both feet. I am the One who loves you completely and wants only the very best for you. I want your life to be an amazing adventure—filled with new things. But first you have to let go of old ways of doing things. Then, grab hold of My hand, and look for all the exciting *new* things I've prepared for you!

READ ON YOUR OWN

Romans 8:38–39; Psalm 56:3–4

Holy Ground

"Do not come any closer," God said. "Take off your sandals,
for the place where you are standing is holy ground."
—Exodus 3:5

At the burning bush, Moses stood on holy ground and heard the very voice of God. And now I am asking you to step onto holy ground and listen to Me!

You don't need a miraculous bush. Just leave behind the cares of this world. For a little while, forget that list of things you're supposed to get done, and just be with Me.

Don't let the world make you feel guilty for our time together. Don't listen to the lie that says you should be busy doing something more productive, something that matters. There is nothing that matters more than spending time with Me—your Lord and Savior. Block out all the noise of the world and be still in My Presence. When you do, you are standing on holy ground.

READ ON YOUR OWN

Isaiah 9:6; Zechariah 9:9; Romans 8:15–16

Think the Thought

But if we confess our sins, he will forgive our sins.
—1 John 1:9 (ICB)

You've heard people say "Walk the walk." This means you should live the way you know is right. Well, now I am asking you to "think the thought." Think the way you know you should—with thoughts centered on Me. When you do, there is no room for thoughts of sin, revenge, hatred, self-pity, or gossip.

I know sometimes a thought just zips into your brain—you don't know where it came from and you don't want it there. Toss it right back out again. I don't hold you responsible for that kind of thought. But when you find yourself holding on to a bad thought—or returning to it over and over again like a familiar song—then you need to bring that thought to Me. Don't try to hide it. Confess it and leave it with Me. Then you can go on your way with a clear mind and a forgiven heart.

READ ON YOUR OWN

Psalm 20:7; Luke 1:79

A Taste of Heaven

*I have told you this so that my joy may be in you
and that your joy may be complete.*
—John 15:11

When you come to Me, be ready. I am a God of unlimited blessings. So get ready to be blessed! Open up your heart and mind to receive more and more of Me. And as you do, I will pour in My blessings of Love, Peace, and Joy—until you are overflowing.

These blessings are only a tiny taste of what waits for you in heaven. The Joy that you have from Me now is like a sparkler in your own backyard, while the Joy of heaven is more like the fireworks in Washington DC on the Fourth of July—but ever so much greater!

I give you real Joy in this world, but in heaven I will make your Joy complete and overflowing.

READ ON YOUR OWN

1 Corinthians 13:12

Listen for My Voice

Love the LORD your God, listen to his voice,
and hold fast to him. For the LORD is your life.
—Deuteronomy 30:20

S top worrying, and listen carefully for My voice. But remember that I speak softly. If your own thoughts are too noisy, you will not hear Me.

I understand that there are many things to think about: school, family, friends, what to wear, what to say, what to do . . . the list goes on and on. All those thoughts start bouncing around in your mind, zigzagging all over the place—until the "noise" they make drowns out My voice.

You'll never hear Me above all that confusion. That is why I gave you a special gift—My Spirit inside you. Ask My Spirit to quiet your thoughts so that you can hear Mine. Then sit peacefully in My Presence—letting My thoughts become yours.

READ ON YOUR OWN

Genesis 1:27; Romans 12:2

Be Real with Me

*I don't call you servants now. A servant does not know
what his master is doing. But now I call you friends because I have
made known to you everything I heard from my Father.*
—John 15:15 (ICB)

I am Lord of lords and King of kings. I am the All-Powerful, Almighty God, Creator of all the universe—and I want to be your Friend.

When you come to Me, don't put on a show. Don't try to use fancy words or rehearse your prayers. When you pretend to be someone that you are not, you hurt Me. I love you just as you are. I know the worst about you, but I also see the very best in you.

When you are with someone you trust completely, you feel free to be yourself. That is one of the greatest things about true friendship. And that is the kind of friendship I want to have with you. Trust Me enough to be real with me.

READ ON YOUR OWN

Revelation 17:14; John 15:13–14

Worship Only Me

You must not make for yourself an idol of any kind or an image of anything in the heavens or on the earth or in the sea.
—Exodus 20:4 (NLT)

Only *I* am God. Only I deserve your worship. Do not devote yourself, your time, or your attention to the things of this world. Do not let them become idols, false gods.

The worship of idols has always been a trap for My people. The ancient Israelites bowed down to carved images and golden statues. But today's idols are harder to spot. They can be other people, possessions, popularity, or success. An idol can be anything that keeps you away from Me.

Don't bow down to the idols of this world. They have no real power. They can't forgive your sins, love you unconditionally, or take you home to heaven. Only *I* can do those things. So worship only Me. And be ready to receive Joy and Peace in My loving Presence.

READ ON YOUR OWN

Exodus 20:5; 2 Samuel 22:29

My Name

Only Jesus has the power to save!
His name is the only one in all the world that can save anyone.
—Acts 4:12 (CEV)

My Name is constantly abused in this world. Some people use it carelessly, without even realizing they are talking about the Lord of lords. Other people use it as a curse word, which is an attack on who I am. Every time My Name is used, it is recorded in heaven.

So when you say My Name in prayer, when you call out My Name in praise, and when you whisper My Name in trust, My aching heart is soothed. All the curses of the world are drowned out by your loving whisper: "Jesus." When you speak My Name in these ways, both you *and* I are blessed.

READ ON YOUR OWN

John 16:24

Constantly and Perfectly Loved

Those who look to him are radiant;
their faces are never covered with shame.
—Psalm 34:5

My Love and salvation are not just waiting for you in heaven; they are here for you now. I want you to know in your heart the Joy of being loved constantly and perfectly—today and every day.

You are so hard on yourself. You judge yourself on how you look, behave, and feel. You look in the mirror, and if you like what you see, you feel a little more worthy of My Love. On good days, it's easier to believe that I love you.

But when you've had a rough day—when you've said and done things you know you shouldn't—you look in the mirror with shame and feel that you're not worthy of My Love. But that is not what I see. When I look at you, I see My beloved child. You are covered with the radiance of My perfect, everlasting Love—no matter what kind of day you've had.

READ ON YOUR OWN

Ephesians 2:7–8; Hebrews 3:1

The Journey

The LORD directs the steps of the godly.
He delights in every detail of their lives. Though they stumble,
they will never fall, for the LORD holds them by the hand.
—Psalm 37:23–24 (NLT)

We are on a wonderful journey together. Though our ultimate goal is heaven, there are lots of adventures all along the way.

There are high points, such as helping a friend learn about Me. There are low points when you struggle with your own questions and doubts. There are crazy twists and turns when things in the world distract you and tempt you. Sometimes the scenery around you is beautiful—and you see Me work in amazing ways. Sometimes the scenery is frightening—like when you must stand alone for what is right. But no matter what part of the journey you are on, I am right there with you.

In good times, we leap up to the mountaintops. In difficult times, I hold your hand and keep you from falling. But at all times, I am beside you as we go along the path of Life.

READ ON YOUR OWN

Psalm 16:11

It's Not a Suggestion

Trust God all the time. Tell him all your problems.
God is our protection.
—Psalm 62:8 (ICB)

Do not worry about tomorrow! This is a command, not a suggestion. I divided time into days for a reason—to make your life easier.

When you pick up the worries of tomorrow and carry them around today, it just makes today harder. And it doesn't help tomorrow at all. Sometimes you carry around the worries of next week, next month, or even next year! You stumble and stagger under the weight of worries that I never meant for you to carry.

Don't just let go of your worries—get rid of them entirely by bringing them to Me. Then concentrate on My Presence with you today. I will give you all that you need, taking care of you—and helping with your problems—today. Then tomorrow, I will do it all over again. *Trust Me.*

READ ON YOUR OWN

Matthew 6:34; 2 Corinthians 12:9

Look Up!

He lifted me out of the slimy pit, out of the mud and mire;
he set my feet on a rock and gave me a firm place to stand.
—Psalm 40:2

Self-pity is a slimy, bottomless pit. Once you fall in, it's almost impossible to get out by yourself. The harder you try to pull yourself out, the farther down you slip. You look down and all you can see is deep darkness.

Don't look down—look up at Me. See My Light, which is still shining on you. See My hand, which is reaching down to you. Reach up in trust and grab My hand. Hold tightly to My promises as I slowly pull you up out of the pit.

I will set your feet on the firm rock of My Love. I will wash away the mud of sin with My forgiveness—and cleanse you with My Peace. I will cover you with the shining clothes of My righteousness. And I will walk with you down the path of Life.

READ ON YOUR OWN

Psalm 40:3; Psalm 42:5; Psalm 147:11

Don't Put Me on Hold

My beautiful one, come with me.
—Song of Songs 2:13

Come away with Me for a while. Take a break from the television, the video games, and the cell phone. Put the world on hold. Most people choose to put *Me* on hold, thinking, *I'll spend time with Jesus later*. But later never seems to come. Be different. Put your time with Me first.

This world makes an idol out of busyness. "The busier you are, the better you must be" is a lie that comes from the world. You can even get too busy with good things. If you are doing so much for your church, your family, and your youth group that you don't have time to spend with Me, then you need to change some things. It won't always be easy, either. But when you choose to come away with Me, you will be blessed with My Love, My Peace, and My Presence. And there is simply nothing better or more important than that.

READ ON YOUR OWN

Luke 10:42

And That Is Faith . . .

*Faith makes us sure of what we hope for and gives us proof
of what we cannot see.*
—Hebrews 11:1 (CEV)

I am nearer than you think. I am present in every moment in your life. Nothing can *ever* separate you from Me.

But I know that sometimes you still feel alone. Even though My Presence is there with you, you don't feel it. Ask Me to open your eyes so that you can "see" Me all around you. I am in the hug of a parent and the smile of a friend. I am in the beauty of a sunset and the majesty of mountains. I am in that soft whisper in the back of your mind that says you are important and loved.

The more you sense My Presence around you, the safer you will feel. I am far more Real than this world that you can see, hear, and touch. And that is faith—knowing and trusting in My Presence as a real fact even though you can't see Me with your eyes.

READ ON YOUR OWN

Acts 17:27–28

Unwanted Feelings

God is light; in him there is no darkness at all.
—1 John 1:5

B ring Me all your feelings, even the ones you wish you didn't have. Fear, anger, jealousy—all those dark feelings disappear if you stay in the Light of My Presence.

Don't try to pretend that you never feel afraid or jealous or angry. Feelings are a part of being human. It is what you *do* with those feelings that makes all the difference. The evil one can use your feelings to try to keep you from doing My will. But don't let fear stop you from stepping out and doing what you know is right. Don't let jealousy blind you to your own talents and blessings. And don't let anger trip you up and cause you to sin.

Trust Me enough to bring all those dark feelings to Me. Spread them out in the Light of My Love, where we will deal with them together.

READ ON YOUR OWN

Ephesians 6:16; 1 John 1:6–7; Isaiah 12:2

Dare to Be Different

Then you will be innocent and without anything wrong in you.
You will be God's children without fault. But you are living with
crooked and mean people all around you. Among them you
shine like stars in the dark world.
—Philippians 2:15 (ICB)

Don't be afraid to be different from other people. I want you to be a bright and shining star in this dark world.

Satan has tricked so many of My children into chasing after the wrong things and admiring the wrong people. Movies and television make heroes out of the bad guys. Cheaters seem to win. And sports stars too often have less-than-shining behavior. Darkness is everywhere.

But I have called you to be different. I made you in My own image, and I hid heaven in your heart. Turn away from the darkness of this world and follow Me. The more time you spend with Me, the brighter your light will shine. And your light will become like a lighthouse that helps others find Me.

READ ON YOUR OWN

Psalm 42:1–2; Psalm 34:5

Plug into Me!

This is what the Lord God, the Holy One of Israel, says:
"If you come back to me and trust me, you will be saved."
—Isaiah 30:15 (ICB)

C ome to Me when you are tired and exhausted. Come to Me when you just need a break. Rest in My Presence. *Rest* is one of My gifts to you. It is not just being still. And it is *not* being lazy. Resting in Me shows that you trust Me enough to relax and lean on Me.

Some people actually run away from Me when they're tired. They think spending time with Me means more work, more responsibilities. So they hide from Me. But the truth is that I am the only place they can truly be recharged. It's a lot like plugging in your cell phone or your video game when the battery is low. Your phone or game waits quietly and then, after a while, it is ready to be used again. When you are tired and your battery is running low, plug into Me by resting in My Presence—and I will give you new strength.

READ ON YOUR OWN

Proverbs 3:5

Live to Please Me

Be careful! When you do good things, don't do them in front of people to be seen by them. If you do that, then you will have no reward from your Father in heaven.
—Matthew 6:1 (ICB)

When your greatest desire is to please Me, then you will be truly free. How? Living to please Me frees you from the phony expectations of this world. Too many of My children do their good deeds to impress their friends, their family, even their church. But if looking good in front of others is your main goal, then you are really only pleasing yourself.

Instead, live to please *Me*. When what you care about the most is pleasing Me, you won't care what other people think. When you believe that I always love you, you can rise above peer pressure. And when you trust that I am always with you, you will have the courage to stand up for what is right.

Live to please Me—and this will make you free.

READ ON YOUR OWN

Ephesians 5:8–10; Matthew 23:8

Be a Light

Let your light shine before men, that they may see your good deeds and praise your Father in heaven.
—Matthew 5:16

This world is full of darkness. But I am the Light of the World. When you choose to follow Me, the Holy Spirit who lives inside you can shine out from your face. Take My Light and carry it into the world around you.

Be My hands by helping others, and love them with My Love. Ask My Spirit to live through you as you make your way through this day. Hold My hand with joy in your heart—trusting that I never leave your side. The Light of My Presence is shining on you. Brighten up the world around you by reflecting this Light—showing *Me* to others.

READ ON YOUR OWN

John 8:12; Matthew 5:14–15;
2 Corinthians 3:18; Exodus 3:14

Be Thankful

Enter his gates with thanksgiving and his courts with praise;
give thanks to him and praise his name.
—Psalm 100:4

I am always with you. But I have given you the freedom to choose whether or not you want to be close to Me. I want you to come to Me because you love Me, not because you have to. So I have placed a "door" between us, and I let you decide whether or not to open it.

One of the best ways to open that door is to *be thankful*. I especially want you to learn to thank Me when times are tough. Your thankfulness tells Me that you trust Me. So when thankful words stick in your throat, check to see if you really do trust Me—even in hard times.

Try seeing how many times you can thank Me each day. This will help you see all the good things I give you—day after day. It will also help you want to *praise My Name!*

READ ON YOUR OWN

1 Thessalonians 5:18

Search for Me

You will search for me. And when you search for me
with all your heart, you will find me!
—Jeremiah 29:13 (ICB)

Do you hear Me? I am calling to you all the time. I speak to you through sights, sounds, thoughts, impressions, Bible verses. There is no limit to the ways that I can speak to you. But you must listen for Me.

When you set your heart on searching for Me, you will always find Me. This world is alive with My Presence. I am there in the beauty of My creation and the songs of birds. I am there in the smiles and laughter of My children. But I am also there in the tough times— in teary faces filled with sadness. I can take the deepest sorrows and make something good come out of them.

Search for Me with all your heart today. I promise that you will find Me!

READ ON YOUR OWN

John 10:27; Romans 8:28

Tune in to Me

Help me obey your commands because that makes me happy.
—Psalm 119:35 (icb)

Most kids don't think of "obeying" and "happy" as being linked together. But they are, especially in your relationship with Me. When you obey Me and let Me have control in your life, you are able to relax and be happy.

You can waste so much time planning your day: trying to figure out what to do—and when to do it. Then, when you think you've got it all just right, something happens. The doorbell rings, a friend calls, you start to feel sick. Your whole plan is thrown off, so you have to start all over again. And you forget all about Me.

There is a much better way. Tune in to Me. I have everything under control: *My* control. Instead of trying to plan everything, let Me show you what to do *now* and *next*. Then you will be free to enjoy Me and the day I have prepared for you.

READ ON YOUR OWN

Psalm 32:8; Psalm 143:8

The Hope of Heaven

Be joyful because you have hope.
Be patient when trouble comes. Pray at all times.
—Romans 12:12 (ICB)

Be full of Joy because you have hope—the hope of heaven.

You and I are on a journey. *Together*. I never leave your side, and I never let go of your hand. When the road gets rough, it is *hope* that helps you look up toward heaven instead of down at your aching feet. When it seems that you are all alone, it is *hope* that reminds you I am still with you. When you just can't take another step, it is *hope* that helps you trust Me to carry you. And when all you can see around you are huge problems, it is *hope* that gives you the courage to keep going.

When you remember that the road we're traveling on is really a highway to heaven, the roughness or smoothness of the road becomes less important to you. I am training you to keep your focus on My Presence with you *and* the hope of heaven.

READ ON YOUR OWN

1 Thessalonians 5:8; Hebrews 6:18–19

Soak in My Love

There is no fear in love. But perfect love drives out fear,
because fear has to do with punishment.
—1 John 4:18

S hut your eyes and imagine you are standing outside in a warm summer rain. The raindrops drench you, soaking you through and through. Let My Love do the same for you. Let it soak through you and wash away hidden fears.

There is no point in trying to hide *anything* from Me. I already know everything about you—and I *still* love you. When you try to hide away parts of yourself, it only hurts you more. Hurts and disappointments can become infected with anger and bitterness. Secret sins can take on a life of their own, controlling you before you even realize it.

Don't close off pieces of yourself from Me. Invite Me in. Show Me all those dark thoughts and feelings. As you spend time with Me, the Light of My Love will chase them away. Rest in My perfect Love—it drives out every fear.

READ ON YOUR OWN

Psalm 139:1–4, 23–24

Wandering Thoughts

And now, dear children, remain in fellowship
with Christ so that when he returns, you will be full of courage
and not shrink back from him in shame.
—1 John 2:28 (NLT)

C ome to Me at all times. I want to be the Center of your life, of all your thoughts.

I know that sometimes you need to think about math or chores or friends. You need to think about what to wear, what to say, and what to do—and that's okay. I can still be the center of your thoughts, even when they are about math. After all, I created numbers. And I can be the center of your thoughts as you consider whether what you're wearing, saying, and doing are pleasing to Me.

But sometimes your thoughts wander to things you shouldn't be thinking about. The question is, how far and how long do you let them wander? When your mind drifts away, My Spirit gives you a little tug—telling you to return to Me. Don't ignore the Spirit's tug. Come back to Me!

READ ON YOUR OWN
Hebrews 6:19; Matthew 22:37

The Beauty of Creation

*Holy, holy, holy is the L*ORD *Almighty;*
the whole earth is full of his glory.
—Isaiah 6:3

The whole of creation declares that I am God. And the beauty of creation declares My Glory.

Open your eyes to the beauty all around you. See the majesty of the mountains, the power of the ocean waves, the details of the tiniest wildflower, the endless colors of the sunset—and know that I am holy God.

So many people rush past these signs of My Presence without even giving them a second thought. Some people just use beauty to sell their products—forgetting all about Me. But I want you to open your eyes to the glory of My creation. Let this awesome beauty draw you into worshiping Me.

Be glad that I am a holy God who created such a beautiful world. And use the glory of My creation to tell others about Me. The whole earth is full of My shining beauty—*My Glory!*

READ ON YOUR OWN

Psalm 29:2

July 31

With and Within You

*For God wanted them to know that the riches and glory of Christ
are for you Gentiles, too. And this is the secret: Christ lives in you.
This gives you assurance of sharing his glory.*
—Colossians 1:27 (NLT)

Trust Me. Really trust Me, deep down inside. Remember that I live *in* you.

This world is constantly demanding something from you. *Go here. Do this. Be this. Say that.* It can send you spinning around like a top, until you feel dizzy, frazzled, and overwhelmed. Don't get upset with yourself when that happens. You are only human. Just take a deep breath and remind yourself that I am not only right here with you, but I am also inside you.

Let My Presence with *and* within you calm you down. Slow down for a while, and search for Me. Deep inside you—where I live— you can find My Peace.

READ ON YOUR OWN

Matthew 28:20; John 20:19

AUGUST

If a person believes in me, rivers of living water will flow out from his heart. This is what the Scripture says.

—John 7:38 (ICB)

I Will Never Leave You

*No one will be able to stand up against you all the days
of your life. As I was with Moses, so I will be with you;
I will never leave you nor forsake you.*
—Joshua 1:5

Nothing can separate you from My Love. *Nothing*. Not bullies, not tough times, not even Satan himself. I will never leave you.

Most of the misery in this world comes from feeling lonely and unloved. Especially when times are tough, people often feel that I have left them all alone. And that feeling can be even worse than the problems they are facing. But know this: I never leave you—not even for a second. I am constantly watching over you. If you feel alone or frightened, ask Me to comfort you with My Presence. Then repeat these promises to yourself: "Nothing can separate me from Your Love, Jesus. . . . You will never leave me."

READ ON YOUR OWN

Romans 8:38–39; Isaiah 49:15–16

The Gift of Your Time

You always gave him blessings.
You made him glad because you were with him.
—Psalm 21:6 (ICB)

This world is obsessed with action. Action heroes, action movies, action adventures. You have to be busy. You have to be on the go—all the time. There is no time to just sit and be still. At least, that's what the world tells you.

But when you come to Me, you are *not* just sitting and being still. You are doing the most important thing of all—letting Me be Lord of your life. As you spend time with Me, My blessings flow over you like streams of living water. I give you blessings of Peace, Love—and the sheer Joy of being in My Presence.

I—your Lord and God—am also blessed by our time together. So bring Me the gift of your time.

READ ON YOUR OWN

John 7:38; Psalm 103:11

August 3

Sticks and Stones

When you talk, do not say harmful things.
But say what people need—words that will help others become
stronger. Then what you say will help those who listen to you.
—Ephesians 4:29 (ICB)

The saying, "Sticks and stones may break my bones, but words will never hurt me," just simply isn't true. Words can cut deeper than any knife. And the wounds they leave behind may never heal.

The world praises people who say "clever" things—even if they embarrass and hurt others. But that is *not* the kind of person I want you to be. Your words are powerful tools. I want you to use them to build up those around you, not tear them down.

I know you get angry and frustrated at times, but don't say the first thing that pops into your mind. Pray first! Before you pick up the phone, pray. Before you answer someone else's angry words, pray. Before you say *anything*, pray! A simple, split-second prayer—"Help me, Jesus"—is all it takes to put your words under My control.

READ ON YOUR OWN

Proverbs 12:18; James 1:19

The Way

Jesus answered, "I am the way and the truth and the life."
—John 14:6

Hold My hand and walk with Me through this day. Together, we will enjoy all the good things that this day holds. And together we will find a way through the difficult things.

I am not only your constant Companion; I am also your Guide. I know every step of the path you are on, and I will guide you—all the way to heaven.

As we walk along, be on the lookout for all the blessings I have prepared just for you: beautiful scenery, exciting adventures, cozy spots for resting when you are tired, and much more.

There's no need to wonder whether or not you are going the right way. I *am* the Way. As long as you stay close to Me, you are sure to be going the right way. Don't worry about what's on the path up ahead. Just enjoy walking with Me today.

READ ON YOUR OWN

Colossians 4:2

A Child of the King

*And the Spirit himself joins with our spirits to say
that we are God's children.*
—Romans 8:16 (ICB)

You are a child of God. A child of the King. A member of My royal family. My own brother or sister. But does the world know it?

You are a child of God on Sunday morning, but whose are you the rest of the week? You are a child of God at church camp, but whose are you at the basketball game? You are a child of God as you lead a prayer, but whose are you when you're deciding what movie to see with your friends?

I want the world to look at you, at what you do and say, and know that you are Mine—whether it's Sunday, Tuesday morning, or Friday night.

Come to Me each morning so that I can prepare you for your day. Ask Me to help you live the day as a royal child of the King. Never forget who you are and Whose you are!

READ ON YOUR OWN

Psalm 37:7; Romans 8:17; 1 Peter 2:9

First, You Must Trust Me

He makes me like a deer, which does not stumble.
He helps me stand on the steep mountains.
—Psalm 18:33 (ICB)

You've seen a deer leaping through the forest—at least on television or in a movie. But have you ever seen one stumble? You've seen goats balanced on bits of rock on steep mountainsides. But have you ever seen one fall?

When you trust in Me, I can make you as surefooted as the deer—so that you don't stumble as you face this life's problems. And I can help you stand on the steep mountainsides of faith without slipping into sin. But first, you must trust Me.

So when everything seems to be going all wrong, stop. Take a deep breath. Tell Me that you trust Me. And tell Me about everything that is upsetting you. Then, leave all your troubles in My hands. Stay in touch with Me through short, simple prayers—thanking Me, trusting Me. Be happy in Me, because I am making you like *a deer that doesn't stumble*.

READ ON YOUR OWN

Job 13:15; Habakkuk 3:17–19

The Whys and Hows

*Therefore, since we have been made right
in God's sight by faith, we have peace with God because
of what Jesus Christ our Lord has done for us.*
—Romans 5:1 (NLT)

You want to understand everything. Why the sky is blue, how your mind works, why bad things happen, and why boys and girls act the way they do. You think if you can understand the whys and hows of things, you can control them—and then you'll have peace. But the problem is that as soon as you figure out one set of things, another set pops up for you to figure out. If you count on your own understanding to give you peace, then you will never really be peaceful.

Instead of searching for the whys and hows, search for *Me*. My Presence and My Peace go together, so when you find Me you also find My Peace.

Put your faith in Me, not in your ability to figure everything out. Besides, I already have everything all figured out.

READ ON YOUR OWN

Proverbs 3:5–6; 2 Thessalonians 3:16

Rock or Sand?

*Anyone who hears and obeys these teachings of mine is like
a wise person who built a house on solid rock. Rain poured down,
rivers flooded, and winds beat against that house. But it did not fall,
because it was built on solid rock.*
—Matthew 7:24–25 (CEV)

The wise man who builds his house on the rock is able to get safely through the storms. And the foolish man who builds his house on the sand—well, his house goes *splat!*

But sometimes in this world, it can be tough to figure out what is rock and what is sand. The world tells you first one thing and then another. Sometimes your teachers say one thing and your parents say another. How can you know what is rock and what is sand?

I am the Rock. Come to Me in prayer, and I will show you what is true, what can be trusted, what is real. Ask My Spirit to guide you as you study My Word. Anything that does not agree with My Word is sand and should not be trusted. Build your house upon the Rock of My Word. And then trust that I will help you stand firm when the storms come—because I will.

READ ON YOUR OWN

Psalm 42:7; Psalm 95:1–2

The Price I Paid

*I am overwhelmed with joy in the L*ORD *my God!*
For he has dressed me with the clothing of salvation
and draped me in a robe of righteousness.
—Isaiah 61:10 (NLT)

C lothes can be very expensive. Getting those jeans with just the right label on them, or that shirt with just the right logo, can cost a lot! But that is nothing compared to the cost of the clothing I have for you—the clothing of salvation.

How much did I have to pay for this clothing? The price was astronomical—out of this world. I paid My life, My own blood. The price was so high that you could never earn enough to buy it for yourself. But it is My free gift to you. This clothing was tailor-made just for you. See how perfectly it fits; it covers over all your flaws. Feel how wonderfully soft its fabric of forgiveness is. See how its length of Love covers you from head to toe.

Wrap yourself in this clothing of salvation—and never take it off. It is My gift to you, made for you even before the creation of the world.

READ ON YOUR OWN

2 Corinthians 5:21; Ephesians 4:22–24

Use Your Time Wisely

So be very careful how you live. Do not live like those who are not wise. Live wisely. I mean that you should use every chance you have for doing good, because these are evil times.
—Ephesians 5:15–16 (ICB)

U se your time wisely. You hear that a lot—from parents and teachers. They usually mean that they want you to get busy and get your work done.

I also want you to use your time well. Each day contains only twenty-four hours; that is 1,440 minutes, or 86,400 seconds. And once those hours, minutes, and seconds are gone, you can never get them back again. So what will you do with today? Surf the Internet, chat with friends, loaf on the couch? Or make the most of every opportunity I give you?

Spend time with Me—in My holy Presence. When you live close to Me, filling your mind with Scripture, I show you how to use your time wisely. I also show you the way you should go—lighting up the path I want you to take. My Word and My Presence are lights for your path.

READ ON YOUR OWN

Psalm 119:105

August 11

What Are You Waiting For?

God is wonderful and glorious.
I pray that his Spirit will make you become strong followers
and that Christ will live in your hearts because of your faith.
—Ephesians 3:16–17 (CEV)

Come to Me. Come to Me. Come to Me. I speak to you in holy whispers, inviting you to come near. Some people think it is hard to approach Me. They believe they must be perfect first. They must have it all together before they can come into My holy Presence. But this is not true.

You don't have to work hard at coming close to Me. Actually, My Love for you is like a strong magnet—pulling you toward Me. All you have to do is trust Me enough to let this powerful Love draw you to Me.

While you are with Me, My Spirit will go to work in you, helping you know in your heart how wide and long and high and deep is My Love for you. Your hurts will be comforted, your fears will be sent away, and your faith will be strengthened. What are you waiting for? Come to Me.

READ ON YOUR OWN

Revelation 22:17; John 6:37; Ephesians 3:18–19

Like a Candle

He will not crush the weakest reed or put out a flickering candle.
—Isaiah 42:3 (NLT)

At times you feel so weak and tired that you just don't know if you have the energy to keep going. You feel like the flame of a candle that is flickering and about to burn out.

Perhaps you think about coming to Me, but you are afraid I will demand something else of you. And you are just so tired. Or perhaps you worry that I will see your weakness as a lack of faith. So you avoid Me.

It's okay to be tired. It's okay to be weak. I understand how difficult things have been. I don't want to judge you. I just want to wrap you up in My everlasting arms and let you rest. Forget about the world, forget the things you need to do, forget the pressures—just come to Me and rest.

READ ON YOUR OWN

Isaiah 54:10; Romans 8:26

August 13

Enjoy Life!

A thief comes to steal and kill and destroy.
But I came to give life—life in all its fullness.
—John 10:10 (ICB)

Life is My gift to you—enjoy it! I came to this earth so that you could live your life to the fullest, not just endure it. I came to take away your sins, to be your guiding Light, and to give you My unconditional Love.

Don't walk around with your head down, trying to "just get through" your day so that you can get up tomorrow and do it all over again. That is what the evil one wants—a dull, tiring life with no joy.

I want every day to be a delight as you live in My Presence and discover My blessings. Yes, there will be problems, and some days will be tough. But when the rain comes, choose to look for the rainbows. Choose to enjoy life, and let the world see *Me* through your Joy!

READ ON YOUR OWN

Matthew 1:23; John 10:11

Rock-Solid

*Long ago you laid the foundation of the earth
and made the heavens with your hands. They will perish, but you
remain forever; they will wear out like old clothing. . . . But you are
always the same; you will live forever.*
—Psalm 102:25–27 (NLT)

This world is constantly changing—time passes, seasons change, people change. Even your body is constantly changing and growing. Nothing on this earth stays the same. But *I* never change. I am always the same—yesterday, today, and forever.

Because I never change, you can always count on Me. Friends may move away; you may switch churches or schools; homes can be destroyed. Sometimes it can feel like your life has been turned completely upside down. When that happens, come to Me. I am rock-solid. You never have to be afraid, because I am always with you and I never change.

READ ON YOUR OWN

Revelation 1:8; Hebrews 13:8; Psalm 48:14

The Position of Your Heart

Morning, noon, and night I cry out in my distress,
and the LORD hears my voice.
—Psalm 55:17 (NLT)

I am the God of all time and of all that is. And I am waiting to hear from you—morning, noon, and night.

Don't just pray to Me in the quiet of the morning. Don't just pray to Me at church or when things are going well. And don't just pray to Me with your head bowed and your eyes closed. Talk to Me every day, at any time, in any place and situation—in class, on the soccer field, while practicing piano or doing homework or texting your friends. Pray when you're in trouble and when you're happy. Time with Me is what matters, not what time it is.

You can talk to Me lying down, sitting up, or with arms stretched up to heaven. Your eyes can be opened or closed. I don't care about the position of your body—I care about the position of your heart. And when your heart is seeking Me, I will hear you.

READ ON YOUR OWN

Psalm 32:6; Psalm 62:8

Focusing Your Thoughts

*Fix your thoughts on what is true, and honorable,
and right, and pure, and lovely, and admirable. Think about
things that are excellent and worthy of praise.*
—Philippians 4:8 (NLT)

S tart your morning with Me. Resist that urge to roll over for just a few more minutes of sleep. Don't fill your room with music or television just yet. Take a few moments to center your thoughts on Me. And let Me fill you with My Joy and Peace.

Then as you go through your day, keep your thoughts focused on Me and My blessings. Pay attention to the things that are best—the things that are worth taking time for—like a true friend, the honor of a grandparent, the pure innocence of a baby, or the loveliness of My creation. Whatever is excellent and good, notice these things and praise Me for them. They are My blessings for you this day.

READ ON YOUR OWN

Isaiah 40:31; Psalm 27:4

One Word

*At the name of Jesus every knee should bow, in heaven
and on earth and under the earth, and every tongue confess
that Jesus Christ is Lord.*
—Philippians 2:10–11

S ome days leave you feeling like Dorothy, spinning around in the middle of a tornado and terrified that you are going to fall at any moment. When that happens, whisper My Name.

Jesus.

That one simple word will help you remember that I am right beside you. One simple word declares that you *know* I am Lord of all and in control of all. One word opens your heart to My Power and Peace in the middle of the storm.

Always remember . . . I'm only one word away.

READ ON YOUR OWN

Isaiah 43:1

Expect the Impossible

He who dwells in the shelter of the Most High
will rest in the shadow of the Almighty.
—Psalm 91:1

Expect troubles—they are just part of living in this world. Stop trying to figure out a way to avoid every problem. An easy life is not the answer. An easy life tricks you into forgetting that you need Me. But everyone needs Me. When you come to Me for help—when you depend on Me—I give you the power to live above your problems.

But don't just expect troubles; expect the impossible too. There will be times when you have no idea what to do, when you can't possibly handle the situation you're facing. Don't try to run away from this situation. It's actually the best place to find Me in all My Power and Glory.

When you see armies of problems marching toward you, cry out to Me! Let Me fight for you. And watch Me work for you, as you rest in the shadow of My Almighty Presence.

READ ON YOUR OWN

Revelation 19:1

August 19

I Am Calling You

*Be still before the L*ORD *and wait patiently for him.*
—Psalm 37:7

I am constantly calling you—calling you to live close to Me.

I know how very much you need Me. I can read your thoughts, and I see how empty they are when they wander away from Me. Come to Me. I will give you rest for your soul, and I will refresh your mind and body.

As you learn to find your joy in Me, the joys of this world—video games, computers, and cell phones—seem less important. Knowing Me—truly knowing Me—is like having a fountain of Joy within you. This fountain flows from Me all the time, so My Joy can be with you even when you're facing problems.

Spending time in My Presence keeps you connected to Me. While you wait with Me, I show you all that I have to offer. If you feel empty or distant from Me, simply bring your attention back to Me. This will keep you close to Me throughout the moments of your life.

READ ON YOUR OWN

Psalm 131:2; Psalm 21:6

The One Who Heals

He forgives all my sins and heals all my diseases.
—Psalm 103:3 (NLT)

I am a God who heals. I heal hurt bodies, troubled minds, aching hearts, messed-up lives, and difficult relationships.

When you come into My Presence, the healing begins. Whether you ask for it or not, My Spirit goes to work in your life. But when you come to Me in prayer *and* ask for My healing, amazing things can happen. Remember that I am a God who can do awesome things! Nothing is too difficult for me.

I don't heal *all* the hurts and troubles in a person's life. Why? Because it is those very problems that keep you close to Me. They are the things that help you grow—teaching you to depend on Me more and more. Even My servant Paul was told, "My grace is enough for you," when he asked to be healed.

While I may not take away every hurt, I will *always* give you what you need to live joyfully—in spite of the hurts. Just ask.

READ ON YOUR OWN

James 4:2; 2 Corinthians 12:7–9; Matthew 7:7

I've Got Plans for You

O LORD, God of Israel, there is no God like you in all of heaven above or on the earth below. You keep your covenant and show unfailing love to all who walk before you in wholehearted devotion.
—1 Kings 8:23 (NLT)

Wait with Me for a while. There is so much that I want to tell you. I have great plans for you. I have all the details worked out. You are walking along the path I have chosen for you. Just follow Me, and I'll show you what to do.

Sometimes you'll feel that you aren't good enough or brave enough to carry out My assignment. But you're looking at your imperfections. I am looking at My Power—*that* makes you good enough and brave enough.

Sometimes My plan will call for you to stand out from the crowd. Don't be afraid to be different; it doesn't matter what other people think. Just stay on the path of Life with Me—trusting Me with all your heart.

READ ON YOUR OWN

Galatians 5:22–23

Shout It Out Loud

Submit yourselves, then, to God.
Resist the devil, and he will flee from you.
—James 4:7

The devil is like a playground bully. He likes to push around those who are feeling weak. He will shove you with a lie, telling you that you're not good enough. He'll attack you with your secret fears, and kick you when you're down.

When you start to feel lonely or afraid or worthless, call out My Name. Tell Me you trust Me. Speak out loud, if you are in a place where you can do that. If not, even a whisper will do. The devil will know that you are not alone—that I am by your side, fighting for you. And then, like the cowardly bully that he is, he will run away.

Chase him away with songs and prayers of praise. Strengthen yourself with My promises—I am always with you; you can do all things with My help; you are My own special creation. Stay close to Me, because the devil will be back—and together we will chase him away again.

READ ON YOUR OWN

Romans 8:1–2; Isaiah 12:2

Give Your Loved Ones to Me

Now I know that you fear God, because you have not
withheld from me your son, your only son.
—Genesis 22:12

It is important to love those around you. In fact, My second greatest command is to love your neighbors as you love yourself. But you must never forget My greatest command—to love Me with all your heart, soul, mind, and strength. Only *I* am God. And only I am worthy of worship.

Love your family, love your friends—but don't worship them. Don't let your love for them crowd out your love for Me. And don't let a person become the center of your life.

Abraham had waited so long for a son. When Isaac finally came, Abraham was in danger of worshiping his son. I tested Abraham, and—as hard as it was—Abraham trusted Me to take care of Isaac. And I did.

Trust Me to take care of your loved ones. They are safe with me. My Presence never leaves them—just as I never leave *you*.

READ ON YOUR OWN

Genesis 22:9–11; Ephesians 3:20; Exodus 33:14

An Open Book

Lord, even before I say a word,
you already know what I am going to say.
—Psalm 139:4 (ICB)

I am all around you. I am nearer than you dare to believe—closer even than the air you breathe. I know every thought before you think it, every word before you say it. So you can see how silly it is to try to hide anything from Me!

You may be able to fool your parents, your teachers, and your friends. But you can never fool Me. I can read you like an open book. I know every secret, every sin. But I don't say this to make you afraid, or to make you feel guilty or ashamed. I say this so that you will *never* feel unloved or lonely again.

Listen carefully as I say this: I know everything about you—and still I will *never* leave you, and I will *never* stop loving you. I have removed all your sins so that you can be this close to Me.

READ ON YOUR OWN

Psalm 139:1–3; Ephesians 2:13; 2 Corinthians 5:21

August 25

The Temple of God

*Don't you know that you yourselves are God's temple
and that God's Spirit lives in you?*
—1 Corinthians 3:16

In order to come into My Presence, the people of Bible times had to travel to the temple, a building of wood and stone in Jerusalem. Even there they were separated from My Presence in the Holy of Holies by a curtain, and they needed priests to speak for them.

But I came to earth to change all that. When I died, the curtain was ripped in two, and there was no longer a separation between Me and My children. And when I left this earth, after My resurrection, I gave you the most wonderful of gifts: I gave you the Holy Spirit to live within you.

Your body is now My temple. You don't have to travel to a faraway city to find Me. And you don't need a priest. You only need to be still and quiet in My Presence. Nothing can separate you from Me!

READ ON YOUR OWN

Exodus 3:14; Psalm 25:14–15

Messy Days

Do not let your hearts be troubled and do not be afraid.
—John 14:27

The world around you is a mess. Crime, wars, drugs—there's bad news every time you turn on the television. And sometimes that mess invades your day. A friend betrays you, something is stolen out of your locker, or someone you know is hurt. But what is happening around you doesn't have to shake you up.

Trust Me—even in the midst of a messy day. When you start to feel stressed, stop focusing on the problems. Instead, reach out to Me. Let Me show you things from My point of view. Remember that My Peace—the Peace that I give you—isn't affected by the mess of this world.

Don't be afraid and don't be troubled. Seek My Face, and I will lift you up above the mess.

READ ON YOUR OWN

John 16:33; Psalm 105:4

Autopilot

Your word is a lamp to my feet and a light for my path.
—Psalm 119:105

Sometimes you can get into a rut, doing the same things day after day. Your brain goes on autopilot, and you don't even think about what you're doing. Letting your brain go on autopilot is an invitation for the devil to slip into the pilot's seat. Before you know it, he'll have you pointed in completely the wrong direction—with lots of terrible detours and trouble along the way.

Kick the devil out of the pilot's seat, and put *Me* in it. Focus your thoughts on Me, and I'll set you back on the right course.

The next time you feel your brain slipping into autopilot, reach for Me and My Word. Let Me put the sparkle of adventure back into your days—lighting up your path.

READ ON YOUR OWN

Psalm 63:7–8

The Light of the Son

The city does not need the sun or the moon to shine on it.
The glory of God is its light, and the Lamb is the city's lamp.
—Revelation 21:23 (ICB)

I came to this earth to give Light to the world. It's different from the sun's light, which makes the trees and plants grow. The Light of My Love shines brighter than any sun ever could.

The Light of My Presence that you see now is only a hint of what heaven will be like. I cannot show you all of My Light now; it would blind you. But in heaven you will be able to see the fullness of My Glory. My Light shines so brightly in heaven that there is no need for a sun, moon, or stars. My Light chases away all the darkness.

I can also chase away the darkness from your life. Just spend time with Me each day, letting My Light soak into your soul. This will help you look forward to seeing the Light of heaven—where you will see Me in all My Glory.

READ ON YOUR OWN

Psalm 4:6–8

Before You Work

Depend on the Lord in whatever you do. Then your plans will succeed.
—Proverbs 16:3 (ICB)

I know that you have a lot to do today. Instead of just jumping in, I want you to try something different: *Wait before you work.*

Put aside all the things you have to do and refuse to worry about what time it is. Don't even look at the clock. By waiting with Me before you start your day, you are saying that you trust Me to be in complete control. This simple act of faith is noticed in heaven—with Joy. And powers of darkness are weakened by your trusting attitude. Then, when it is time to start working, I will show you which way to go.

Depend on Me to help you decide what really needs to be done today, so you can save time by doing only the important things. This way, you can do less but get more of the important things done—by *waiting before working.*

READ ON YOUR OWN

Luke 12:22–26; Ephesians 6:12

The God Who Forgives

Where can I go to get away from your Spirit?
Where can I run from you? . . . If I rise with the sun in the east, and
settle in the west beyond the sea, even there you would guide me.
With your right hand you would hold me.
—Psalm 139:7–10 (ICB)

There is no place where you cannot find Me.

There is no problem that can keep Me away from you.

You cannot run away from Me, and you cannot chase Me away from you.

I am the God who forgives. When you mess up, I am there to pick you up, dust you off, forgive you, and cover you with My Love.

I did not come to earth to judge you and condemn you. I came to make you free. Yes, I see your mistakes and your sins and rebellion. But I also see My precious child—forgiven and shining with My righteousness. You are My delight, and I sing over you with Love.

READ ON YOUR OWN

Genesis 16:7–14; Zephaniah 3:17

Have You Heard?

*Do you not know? Have you not heard? The L*ORD *is the everlasting God, the Creator of the ends of the earth. He will not grow tired or weary, and his understanding no one can fathom.*
—Isaiah 40:28

Have you heard? I use your weaknesses to make you stronger.

That sounds backward, doesn't it? The world says that the strong are those who don't have any weaknesses; the strong are the people who do it all on their own, who rely on their own strength and smarts. But I tell you that there will come a time when those people will run out of strength and their own wisdom will fail them.

My Way is different. I use your unexpected problems to urge you to seek My guidance. Your weaknesses are not punishment. Rather, struggles are a gift that helps you learn to depend on Me. I want you to trust Me and lean on Me—rather than on your own understanding.

When you lean on Me, you are truly strong. Because My Strength never runs out, and My wisdom never fails.

READ ON YOUR OWN

James 4:13–15; Proverbs 3:5; Isaiah 40:29–31

SEPTEMBER

I am the Light of the world; he who
follows Me will not walk in the
darkness, but will have the Light of life.

—John 8:12 (NASB)

Search for Me

*From there you will seek the L*ORD *your God, and you will find Him*
if you search for Him with all your heart and all your soul.
—Deuteronomy 4:29 (NASB)

I want you to search for Me—not just once in a while, not just on Sundays, and not just when you need My help. I want you to look for Me at all times.

And I want you to search with all your heart and soul—not just because you think you should, or because someone told you to. Look for Me with everything that is in you because you want to find Me.

When you search for Me with all your heart and all your soul, you *will* find Me—and you will enjoy Love, Joy, and Peace in My Presence. I promise.

Seek Me in good times; seek Me in hard times. And you will find Me watching over you all the time.

READ ON YOUR OWN

Hebrews 10:23; Psalm 145:20

An Adventure with Me

*On that day you will realize that I am in my Father,
and you are in me, and I am in you.*
—John 14:20

Living your life while depending on Me is a great adventure. Most people—grown-ups and kids alike—scurry around trying to do things their own way. Some are huge successes; others fail miserably. But both miss out on what life is supposed to be—*an adventure with Me.*

When you give control of your life to Me, I open your eyes so that you can see Me at work in the world. Where others see "coincidences," you see My wonderful work—even miracles at times. And where others see only an everyday happening, you see Me.

Live each day just watching for what I will do next. You are in Me, and I am in you—and through Me you learn to truly live. This is the amazing adventure I offer you.

READ ON YOUR OWN

2 Corinthians 12:9–10; Acts 17:28; Colossians 2:6–7

September 3

Never Changing

God is not a God of confusion but a God of peace.
—1 Corinthians 14:33 (ICB)

This world is full of confusion. So many things compete for your attention—school, sports, church, family, and on and on. You are constantly bombarded with more and more interruptions—from the radio, television, Internet, your cell phone and iPod. In this world, there is no lasting peace.

Life on planet earth has changed so much since I first gave the command to *be still and know that I am God*. But I have not changed, and My ways have not changed. Come to Me with all your confusion, even if it's over something small. Tell Me everything. I will still your mind and help you sort everything out. I will take away the confusion and replace it with My Peace.

READ ON YOUR OWN

Psalm 46:10; Luke 10:39–42

JESUS CALLING FOR KIDS

I Am the Light

I am the light of the world. The person who follows me will never live in darkness. He will have the light that gives life.
—John 8:12 (ICB)

I created Adam and Eve to walk side by side with Me. I loved walking and talking with them in the garden, before the evil one tricked them. Ever since that time, man has had a huge, dark emptiness in his heart—an emptiness that only My Presence can fill.

Some people try to fill that hole with the things of this world—popularity, money, even drugs or alcohol. Other people try good things—such as teaching others or being a volunteer—hoping that goodness will make them whole. But no matter how good you are, only *I* can fill that emptiness.

Live close to Me. The Garden of Eden is no more, but the garden of your heart is alive and well. Walk with Me in the garden of your heart—letting Me fill the emptiness. In this way I can live in the world through you! Together we will push back the darkness, for I am the Light of the world.

READ ON YOUR OWN

Psalm 32:7; Genesis 3:8–9

No Other Friend Like Me

There is no greater love than to lay down one's life for one's friends.
—John 15:13 (NLT)

I am your best Friend, *and* I am your King.

My friendship is practical and down-to-earth. As your Friend, I am always here to listen and to help. Together we will face whatever each day brings: pleasures, hardships, adventures, disappointments.

But as your heavenly King, our friendship opens up so many more possibilities. As King, I can create something wonderful out of the ashes of lost dreams, Joy out of sorrow, and Peace out of problems.

And it's all because I love you. My Love for you is so great that I gave up heaven to come to earth as a helpless baby. It is so great that I lived in the dust and sin of this world. And it is so great that I died on the cross to save your soul. There is no other friend like Me!

READ ON YOUR OWN

John 15:14–15; Isaiah 61:3; 2 Corinthians 6:10

Depend on Me

Finally, be strong in the Lord and in his mighty power.
—Ephesians 6:10

I want to do it by myself."

You've heard that said before. You've said it yourself. And for some things that is good. You *do* need to learn how to make your bed, clean up your room, and do long division.

But there are other things that you shouldn't do by yourself—like choose the direction of your life. If you try that on your own, you can end up in some lonely and terrible places. You can end up weak, frightened, and lost.

Don't go it alone. Depend on Me. I know your strengths and your weaknesses. And I know the future. Using this knowledge, I have created the perfect plan for your life. You don't have to do it all by yourself. Let My Strength make you strong, and let My Wisdom lead the way.

READ ON YOUR OWN

John 15:5; Genesis 1:26–27

I Set You Free

*I am not judged guilty because in Christ Jesus the law
of the Spirit that brings life made me free. It made me free
from the law that brings sin and death.*
—Romans 8:2 (ICB)

I did not come to this earth to make you feel guilty. I came to free you from guilt.

And I don't like it when others use guilt to get you to follow Me. I want you to come to Me out of love—because you want to be in My Presence.

It is true. I know every mistake you have ever made, every sin you have ever done. But when you come into My Presence, I don't see your sins; I see My beloved child. When you ask Me to forgive you, My grace washes all your sins completely away. Not only do I forgive them, but I forget all about them. I set you free.

READ ON YOUR OWN

Isaiah 61:10; Romans 8:1; Psalm 103:11–12

Weak and Weary

I will give rest and strength to those who are weak and tired.
—Jeremiah 31:25 (ICB)

S ome days you just don't feel good. You didn't get enough sleep, you feel a cold coming on, or maybe you overdid it a little yesterday.

When your body is feeling tired and weak, that is when you need Me the most. Your defenses are down, and the devil is just waiting to trip you up. You're so tired, he tricks you into saying words you never meant to say—like smarting off to your mom or dad. And when you're weak, he talks you into taking shortcuts that are bad for you—like borrowing a friend's homework to copy.

When you feel weak and weary, don't give up or give in. Come to Me. Ask for an extra dose of My Strength. Ask Me to protect you from Satan's attacks. And if you've already fallen into one of the evil one's traps, call out to Me. I'll pull you out of the trap and help you through the day.

READ ON YOUR OWN

Psalm 42:5; 2 Corinthians 13:4

September 9

From Point A to Point B

Show me the right path, O Lᴏʀᴅ; point out the road for me to follow. Lead me by your truth and teach me, for you are the God who saves me. All day long I put my hope in you.
—Psalm 25:4–5 (ɴʟᴛ)

In math class, you learn that the shortest distance between two points is a straight line. So let's pretend that you are at point A and I am at point B. The quickest way for you to get from A to B—to *Me*—is through the straight line of unwavering trust.

The key is *unwavering*. It means trusting Me constantly, no matter what. Because when your trust wavers—when sometimes you trust Me a lot, other times only a little, and other times you completely forget Me—then your straight line of trust starts to have lots of twists and turns. You can still reach Me—eventually. But you will have wasted a lot of time and gone through a lot of unnecessary trouble. When you realize that your trust has wavered, just whisper, "I trust You, Jesus." And I will draw you back onto the right path with Me.

Trust in Me with all your heart, and I will make your path straight.

READ ON YOUR OWN

Isaiah 26:4; Psalm 9:10; Proverbs 3:5–6

I Promise You

*"The mountains may disappear, and the hills may come to an end.
But my love will never disappear. My promise of peace will not come
to an end," says the Lord who shows mercy to you.*
—Isaiah 54:10 (ICB)

I am always here for you.

Once you have trusted Me as your Savior, I never leave your side.
There may be times when you feel far away from Me. But that is
just a feeling; it is *not* fact. You can find the truth in My promises
throughout the Bible. I promised Jacob that I would never leave
him. I promised Joshua the same thing. And My last promise
was to all of My followers: I am with you always, until the end of
time. I promised them, and I promise you.

The mountains may disappear and the hills may come to an
end, but even then I will never leave you. My Love lasts forever;
it never fails.

READ ON YOUR OWN

Genesis 28:15; Joshua 1:5; Matthew 28:20

The Secret of Being Happy

I have learned the secret of being happy
at any time in everything that happens.
—Philippians 4:12 (ICB)

Choose to be happy in Me—no matter what is going on around you.

Don't wait for everything in your life to be perfect before you decide to be happy. Too many people waste their lives dreaming about the time when they'll finally be happy—when they are out of school, when they can drive, when they have their own job or house, and so on. But while they are daydreaming, life is passing them by. Life is *today*, not "when . . ."

If your life is going great, be happy and enjoy My blessings. If times are tough, be happy because you know these problems will go away. And don't forget this either: You have the promise of a problem-free life in heaven—*forever*—with Me!

Don't wait to be happy. Come to Me and I will show you how to be happy *today*.

READ ON YOUR OWN

Philippians 4:4; Psalm 102:27

I Am Your Best Defense

*We fight with weapons that are different
from those the world uses. Our weapons have power from God.
These weapons can destroy the enemy's strong places.*
—2 Corinthians 10:4 (ICB)

When you sit quietly with Me, trusting Me, it may look like you are doing nothing. But you are really at war. There are great and terrible battles being fought every day in spiritual realms, and your quiet trust makes a difference.

By quietly trusting in Me, you are using some of heaven's greatest weapons. This battle is not fought with guns, tanks, or rockets. This battle is fought with spiritual weapons. The evil one uses fear, loneliness, anger, and shame to attack you. But My weapons are more powerful. Fear is defeated by trust. Loneliness is cast out by My Presence. Anger is erased by My Peace. And shame is driven away by forgiveness. Stay close to Me—I am your best defense against evil.

READ ON YOUR OWN

John 14:27; Isaiah 30:15

Take a Break from Judging

Do not judge, or you too will be judged.
—Matthew 7:1

Y ou can get into a habit of judging. You judge this situation and that situation, this person and that person. You judge yourself. You even judge the weather. So much of your time is spent making judgments—as if that were your main job in life. Actually, your main job is to worship Me. So forget about judging, and just come to Me.

I am the Creator, and you are My creation. I am the Shepherd, and you are My sheep. I am the Potter, and you are My clay. Let Me have My way in your life. It is not your place to judge—not even yourself. Judging is *My* job.

Worship Me as the King of all kings—the King who loved you enough to die for you and save you from judgment.

READ ON YOUR OWN

John 17:3; Romans 9:20–21; 1 Timothy 6:15

Your Secret Mission

Since God has shown us great mercy, I beg you to offer your lives as a living sacrifice to him. Your offering must be only for God and pleasing to him. This is the spiritual way for you to worship.
—Romans 12:1 (ICB)

S acrifice is a difficult word to understand. And it is even more difficult to practice. It means giving up what you want for yourself in order to please or help someone else. In your relationship with Me, it means giving up control of your life—to let Me show you the way *I* want you to live. When you sacrifice your own will to Mine, seeking to please Me, that is worship.

I know that you want to be off on a great adventure for Me. But sometimes the greatest adventures are the ones you don't see. While your daily life may seem routine, your spiritual life can be involved in a huge, secret mission—to climb the mountain of trust and find the treasure of My Presence. When you live close to Me, you are offering yourself to Me as a living sacrifice. This pleases Me and helps Me turn your routine days into spiritual adventures of worship.

READ ON YOUR OWN

Genesis 2:7; Psalm 89:15; Romans 12:2

You Are Good Enough

May the Lord show you his kindness. May he have mercy on you.
—Numbers 6:25 (icb)

You are good enough for Me to love. Just as you are. You don't have to do anything big or spectacular. You don't have to earn My Love or fight for My attention. All you have to do is lie back, close your eyes, and rest in My Love for you. I will wrap you up in the warm, soft blanket of My unconditional Love, which never ends. I don't want you to worry any more about being good enough to be loved.

Look into My eyes. There is no condemnation there. You have nothing to fear because you are My child—and I took the punishment for *all* your sins. So I'm not thinking about your mistakes or what you should have done or wishing you'd worked harder. When you look into My eyes, you will see only kindness, delight, and unending Love.

READ ON YOUR OWN

John 15:13; Zephaniah 3:17; Numbers 6:26

I Make You Complete

It is worth nothing for a person to have the whole world,
if he loses his soul.
—Mark 8:36 (ICB)

I designed you to need *Me* in order to have a full life. In this world you may have many things—popularity, riches, power, possessions. But unless you have Me, you will always be missing something. Without Me, there is an empty place inside you in this life. And without Me, you would have only darkness in eternity.

Trust that I know what I'm doing—even when I lead you along a path that feels strange. If you follow Me with all your heart, you will discover exciting new things about yourself. I will show you gifts and talents that you never knew you had. And you will become more and more the one I created you to be. My Presence will make you complete.

READ ON YOUR OWN

Psalm 139:13–16; 2 Corinthians 3:17–18

Control Equals Peace

Depend on the Lord. Trust him, and he will take care of you.
—Psalm 37:5 (ICB)

Plan. Plot. Scheme. That is the way this world does things. It's all about control. Control your time, control your money, control the people and events around you—control your life. Control equals peace.

But the thing is, you can never be in complete control. Just when you think you've prepared for every possibility, something unexpected pops up and ruins all your plans. Your parents may say no, the weather may cancel the big game, or sickness may stop you from getting out of bed.

Control *does* equal peace—but only when it's *My* control. Bring Me all your needs, your hopes and fears, and leave them in My care. Depend on Me to do the planning, and I will give you My Peace.

READ ON YOUR OWN

1 Peter 5:6–7; Proverbs 16:9

Working for Me

Work willingly at whatever you do,
as though you were working for the Lord rather than for people.
—Colossians 3:23 (NLT)

Every day you are faced with choice after choice. When you're trying to make decisions, you need a good goal to guide you. So seek to please Me in all your choices—in all that you do.

You know that in order to please Me you need to spend time with Me. Worship, prayer, praise, and Bible study—these are things that make Me smile.

But pleasing Me isn't just about the things you do with Me. It's also about the things you do for Me. From the big things like helping the sick, giving to the poor, and being a friend to the friendless, to the everyday things like emptying the dishwasher for your mom, taking out the trash for your dad, and being respectful—do everything for Me. It may seem like you are working for others, but you are really working for Me. So do the best you can, knowing I'll be with you in all of it.

READ ON YOUR OWN

Matthew 6:33; John 8:29; Colossians 3:24

I Am Life

Do not love the world or the things in the world. If anyone loves the world, the love of the Father is not in him.
—1 John 2:15 (ICB)

There is a battle going on for the control of your mind—a battle between heaven and this world. And the winner is up to you.

The world pulls your thoughts down, away from heaven. It makes you crave fun for the sake of fun. It makes you want to own everything you see. And it tricks you into thinking you're better than others because of the things you have and the things you've done. The world tells you that this is *life*. But the things of this world don't last.

Shut out the world for a while so that you can enjoy My Presence. As you focus on Me, My Spirit fills your mind with Life and Peace.

Yes, you live in this world, but don't let it become your life. *I* am *Life*.

READ ON YOUR OWN

Ephesians 2:6; Psalm 27:8; Romans 8:6; 1 John 2:16–17

Shake It Off

The Lᴏʀᴅ directs our steps,
so why try to understand everything along the way?
—Proverbs 20:24 (NLT)

I have a perfect plan for your life. So trust Me and try to see things from My point of view. When things don't go quite the way you expected, shake them off. Look up at Me, shrug your shoulders, and say with a grin, "Oh, well." Then just let them go— and move on.

This simple act of trust will keep you from weighing yourself down with little frustrations. With enough practice, you will discover that most of the things you worry about just aren't that important. Your energy and time won't be wasted on things that really don't matter—and you'll have the strength to deal with big problems when they do come your way.

You know that thing that's bothering you right now? Shake it off, and let's move on together.

READ ON YOUR OWN

2 Corinthians 4:17–18

Holy Whispers

*After the earthquake came a fire, but the L*ORD *was not in the fire.*
And after the fire came a gentle whisper.
—1 Kings 19:12

I am Almighty God! At My command, the sun exploded into being. Through My powerful words, I shot mountains up into the air, created huge oceans with crashing waves, and filled the world with all kinds of amazing creatures.

Heaven is My throne, and the earth is My footstool. But I choose to make My home in your heart. And I choose to speak to you in gentle whispers. I am the God of all Power, but I am also the God of all Peace and Love. Ask Me to quiet your mind and shut out the noises of this world. Then you can hear My holy whispers—assuring you of My Love.

READ ON YOUR OWN

Isaiah 66:1; Psalm 5:3

Your Strength, Your Song

The Lord is my strength and my song; he has become my salvation.
He is my God, and I will praise him.
—Exodus 15:2

Remember, I am your Strength and your Song.

Some mornings, you feel a little wobbly. You look at the day ahead and think about all you have to do. Then you start to think about tomorrow and next week and even next month. And then you start to feel overwhelmed!

Among all My creatures, human beings are the only ones who can think about the future. This is a special blessing, but it can also be a curse—if you start to worry about future things. Instead, use your wonderful mind to think about *Me*. Because I am your Strength, I can give you strength to handle each task as it comes. And because I am your Song, I can give you Joy as we work together on those tasks.

So relax and enjoy working with Me—your Strength and your Song.

READ ON YOUR OWN

2 Corinthians 10:5; Hebrews 10:23

Be Free

We praise you, Lord God! You treat us
with kindness day after day, and you rescue us.
—Psalm 68:19 (CEV)

I see you carrying around a bunch of burdens: guilt over something you said to your mom or dad, anger at a friend's betrayal, sadness at a disappointment. I did not create you to walk around with such heavy loads. They pull you down and make you stumble.

When you are carrying so much weight, you are much more likely to fall. When you are hauling around guilt and anger, you are much more likely to sin by doing or saying something you shouldn't.

I want you to give your burdens to Me. Just hand them over and don't look back. That's why I died on the cross—to free you from your burdens. Let Me sweep them away with My forgiveness. Let Me set you free!

READ ON YOUR OWN

1 John 1:7–9; 1 John 4:18

Compared to Forever

I know the Lᴏʀᴅ is always with me.
I will not be shaken, for he is right beside me.
—Psalm 16:8 (ɴʟᴛ)

I am much more "real" than this world. This world—and all the things in it—will someday be gone. But I am forever. Once you compare *things* to *forever*, it becomes much easier to shake off today's hurts and disappointments.

Years from now, when you're starting your career, it won't matter that you made a bad grade on a test. But it *will* matter that you kept trying. Twenty or thirty years from now, when you're playing with your own children, it won't matter that you didn't make the team. But it will matter that you cheered on those who did. And an eternity from now, nothing from this life will matter—except that you loved Me and loved other people with My Love.

Don't be shaken by the troubles of this world. One day they will be gone, and I will take you home with me—*forever*.

READ ON YOUR OWN

Psalm 89:15–16; 2 Peter 1:2

September 25

Trust Keeps You Safe

Fearing people is a dangerous trap,
but trusting the LORD means safety.
—Proverbs 29:25 (NLT)

B eing around other people can be scary. What if you say the wrong thing? What if you wear the wrong clothes? What if you don't fit in with the in-crowd? What if you trip and fall—right in the middle of the lunchroom?

Some days are like walking through a minefield. One false step and—BOOM! So you spend your whole day trying to do and say just the right things, hoping to please everyone. You even do and say things you know are wrong, just to fit in. By the end of the day, you're exhausted. And the only thing you've earned is the privilege of getting up and doing it all again tomorrow.

Being afraid of what people think is dangerous. And living to please others can get you into big trouble. Live to please *Me* instead. I will help you make good choices. And I will help you get through the minefield of your day.

Trust Me, and I will keep you safe.

READ ON YOUR OWN

Psalm 23:4; Matthew 7:1–2

The Curtain

And when Jesus had cried out again in a loud voice, he gave up his spirit. At that moment the curtain of the temple was torn in two from top to bottom. The earth shook and the rocks split.
—Matthew 27:50–51

Y ou can live your whole life and never meet the president, the queen of England, or even the governor of your own state. The rulers and royalty of this world prefer to keep themselves separate from "ordinary" people.

But I am the King of the universe, and you can meet with Me *anytime*. You don't need an appointment. You don't need a special invitation. And you don't even have to go anywhere. You can sit in the comfort of your own room and speak directly with the King of kings.

This is My gift to you—bought with My own blood. Before I died on the cross, people were separated from God by a thick curtain in the temple. When I died, that curtain was torn in two. Now I, the King of all kings, am your constant Companion and Friend.

READ ON YOUR OWN

Isaiah 50:4; Isaiah 55:2–3; John 19:30

The Glow of My Presence

I truly believe I will live to see the Lord's goodness.
—Psalm 27:13 (ICB)

I am constantly working in your life, even though you may not realize it. Especially when you are tired or hurt, or the day has had too many troubles, you may not notice Me at all. But I am there.

When you are tired, I am the One who is gently urging you on. When you are hurt, I am the One who is softly whispering, "It's going to be okay." And when you are overwhelmed, I am the One who is running before you, clearing the path of things you just can't face today.

In those times that you have felt the weakest, I have been working the hardest for you. And though you may not see Me right now, one day you will look back and know that I was right there all along, giving you all that you needed. Your memories of those days will be bright with the glow of My Presence.

READ ON YOUR OWN

Deuteronomy 33:27; Psalm 27:14

Unconditionally

Jesus understands every weakness of ours,
because he was tempted in every way that we are. But he did not sin!
—Hebrews 4:15 (CEV)

Remember that the devil is the father of lies. He likes to sneak into your thoughts and whisper lies to you. One of his favorites is to tell you that I don't really love you *unconditionally*. Satan wants you to believe that you have to be good enough to be loved. If you make one little mistake—if you even think about a sin—then surely I won't love you anymore.

That is a lie. I love you, *no matter what*. This world is full of temptations. It's hard to always resist, and it's impossible for you to be perfect. I understand that. I walked on this earth, too, and I was exactly your age once.

But be encouraged: I lived a perfect life in this world and then died to wash away your sins. And I rose from the grave to be your Savior. All because I love you—*unconditionally*. Come close to Me, and I'll wrap you up in My perfect Love.

READ ON YOUR OWN

Ephesians 3:16–19; Hebrews 4:14, 16;
John 8:44; James 4:7–8

My Definition of Wonderful

I praise you because you made me in an amazing and wonderful way.
—Psalm 139:14 (ICB)

I created *you*, not just humans in general. Every detail, every feature of yours, was lovingly and carefully formed by Me. *And you are wonderful!*

This world will tell you that you need to look a certain way, talk a certain way, and live a certain way in order to be wonderful. Just look at any magazine, and you will see the world's definition of wonderful—thanks to digital photography and a few tweaks here and there on the computer. But remember that this world is ruled by the father of lies. And one of his biggest whoppers is that only certain people are truly special.

All My children are wonderful—each in his or her own unique way. Just look in the mirror, and you will see *My* definition of wonderful.

READ ON YOUR OWN

Psalm 34:4–7; 2 Peter 1:16–17; John 17:3

I Already Know

So don't worry about tomorrow, for tomorrow will bring its own worries. Today's trouble is enough for today.
—Matthew 6:34 (NLT)

I am God. I am here, there, and everywhere. All at the same time.

I am God. I am yesterday, today, and tomorrow. All at the same time.

That is how I am able to take care of you completely. I get up with you in the morning, *and* I am already waiting for you on the bus. I eat lunch with you, *and* I already know what you will have for dinner. I go to sleep with you each night, *and* I already know where you will be fifty years from now.

So when I tell you not to worry—that I will take care of you—I mean it! I know what problems you will face tomorrow. I've already seen them, and today I'm preparing you to face them. So leave tomorrow's worries where they belong: in tomorrow. And when you *do* get to tomorrow, I'll already be there—without ever having left your side today.

READ ON YOUR OWN

John 10:10; James 4:13–15

OCTOBER

Come to me, all of you who are tired and have heavy loads. I will give you rest.

—Matthew 11:28 (ICB)

Come to Me

The glorious God is the only Ruler, the King of kings and Lord of lords. . . . God will be honored, and his power will last forever.
—1 Timothy 6:15–16 (CEV)

I am the all-powerful King of kings and Lord of lords—which means I have the Power to take care of you. Not only do I have the Power, but I *want* to take care of you. Will you let Me?

Some people are afraid to come to Me when they're hurting or tired. They're afraid that I will ask even more of them, when they've already worked so hard they can barely move. All of this makes them want to hide from Me.

What I want is to be their *hiding place*—and yours. Let Me heal your hurts and give you a quiet place for your soul to rest. Come to Me, and I will give you rest.

READ ON YOUR OWN

Isaiah 55:8–9; Revelation 2:4; Matthew 11:28

Every Hair on Your Head

Yes, God even knows how many hairs you have on your head.
Don't be afraid.
—Luke 12:7 (icb)

Don't ever forget that I know you better than you know your-self—and far better than anyone else knows you. Your parents, your best friend, your brother or sister cannot be with you at all times. But I am. And at every moment I know your every thought, every feeling, every hope and dream. I know every detail about you—right down to how many hairs you have on your head.

Not only do I know you, but I also understand you. I know all the whys and hows that you can't even put into words. I understand what is inside your heart.

Many people spend their whole lives searching for someone who can truly understand them. But all you have to do is call on My Name—opening your heart to Me. This simple act of faith is all it takes. I understand you perfectly, and I love you forever.

READ ON YOUR OWN

John 1:12; Romans 10:13

Supernatural

I trust in your love. My heart is happy because you saved me.
—Psalm 13:5 (ICB)

When it seems like absolutely everything is going wrong—trust Me. When your life feels more and more out of control—thank Me.

That's not what usually pops into your mind first, is it? When you've missed the bus, lost your best friend, and the dog really did eat your homework—your first response is to complain. That's only natural. But whining and complaining are like jumping on a giant slide. Once you start down, you only go faster and faster—more whining and complaining. And at the bottom of that slide, there's nothing but a big pit of self-pity.

Put on the brakes! Don't do the "natural" thing—do what is *beyond* natural. Do what is *supernatural*. Trusting and being thankful in the middle of a really bad day are supernatural responses, and they unlock My supernatural Power in your life. I'll see you through whatever mess you're in and fill you up with My Peace, which is beyond your understanding.

READ ON YOUR OWN

Ephesians 5:20

My Spirit in You

*Then I will ask the Father to send you the Holy Spirit
who will help you and always be with you.*
—John 14:16 (CEV)

I am the Creator of heaven and earth. I am the Lord of all that is and all that will ever be. I am bigger than all the heavens. But when you choose to become one of My followers, I come to live inside you. Think about that for a moment—about who I am and how big I am. And then rejoice because My Spirit lives in you.

The Holy Spirit is always there to help you—just ask. When everything is going your way and life seems easy, you may be tempted to go it alone. But that is when you are in the greatest danger. The evil one is just waiting for you to let your guard down, to step away from My protection. Ask My Spirit to help you *every* step of the way—during hard times *and* easy times. The Spirit makes you strong.

READ ON YOUR OWN

John 14:17; John 16:7; Zechariah 4:6

October 5

Happiness Versus Joy

Honor and majesty surround him; strength and joy fill his dwelling.
—1 Chronicles 16:27 (NLT)

Happiness and Joy are not the same thing.

Happiness depends on this world, on what is going on around you. Happiness is when you ace the test, or make the winning shot, or you're headed for a vacation at the beach with your best friend. It depends on everything being just right. Happiness is wonderful, but it lasts only a little while.

But *Joy*—true Joy—is something entirely different. Joy doesn't depend on this world, or whether you're having a good day; it depends on *Me*. Joy is knowing that I am in control, that I love you and will take care of you—even when you flunk the test, or make the last out, or your family can't afford a vacation. Stay close to Me, and I'll give you My Joy in every situation.

READ ON YOUR OWN

Habakkuk 3:17–19

The Invisible Shepherd

We walk by faith, not by sight.
—2 Corinthians 5:7 (NKJV)

Be willing to follow wherever I lead you. Follow Me with your whole heart—even when you don't know where I am taking you.

You want to *see*, you want to *know* what's coming so that you can be ready. But that is depending on yourself. Put your faith in Me instead, and I'll make sure you're ready.

You don't know what lies ahead, but *I* know—and that is enough! Some of My best surprises are just around the corner—out of sight but very real. To receive these blessings, you must *walk by faith, not by sight*.

This doesn't mean you close your eyes to what is happening all around you. It means trusting Me—your invisible Shepherd—more than the things that you can see.

READ ON YOUR OWN
Psalm 96:6; John 8:12; Psalm 36:9

Chasing away the Fog

This is the day the LORD has made. We will rejoice and be glad in it.
—Psalm 118:24 (NLT)

Some mornings you wake up and the world is blanketed with a thick fog. As you look out your window, you can trace the outline of the house across the street and perhaps the car out front. But the details are impossible to see.

That is what living with worry and fear is like. They create a fog in your mind and heart that keeps you from seeing Me clearly. But just as the sunlight chases away the morning fog, My Light chases away the fog of fear and worry.

All you have to do is tell Me about your worries and fears, and then leave them with Me. Don't snatch them back again! Trust Me to help you handle everything that happens, knowing it doesn't surprise Me. And count on Me to take care of you. Let My Light chase away the fog. Then go out and live your day in the sunshine of My Love.

READ ON YOUR OWN

1 Peter 5:6–7; 1 Thessalonians 5:18

Unchanging

I have loved you, my people, with an everlasting love.
With unfailing love I have drawn you to myself.
—Jeremiah 31:3 (NLT)

I love you with an everlasting Love. It has no beginning and no end. And it never changes.

It is impossible for you to completely understand My Love. You tend to see Me and My feelings the same way as you see your own. Your feelings change. Friends come and go. Anger can make you feel less love for someone, while happiness can make you feel more. And in the back of your mind, you wonder if I am that way too.

I am not. There is nothing you can do that will change My Love for you. If you mess up, I am sad but I don't love you less. If you do something wonderful for Me, I am happy but I don't love you more. My Love is the same yesterday, today, and forever. And it's bigger and deeper than you could ever imagine! So let Me love you . . . always.

READ ON YOUR OWN

Exodus 15:13; Hebrews 13:8

Tell Me All About It

Do everything without complaining or arguing.
—Philippians 2:14

You have been on a long, difficult journey. Sometimes your energy seems to be almost used up. You've found it hard just to keep going, but you have not let go of My hand. And I am really proud of you for that.

But there is one thing I want you to work on: your complaining. You can talk with Me about *anything*—you can even complain. I understand you better than anyone, so I am the perfect One to vent to. Telling Me your stresses and your problems helps you get a grip on your thoughts. It also helps you see things from My point of view.

But complaining to others is completely different. It can lead to the sins of gossip, anger, and self-pity.

When you need to grouch and grumble, come to Me. Let's talk it out. Spill out all the bad stuff, so I can fill your mind with My thoughts—and your heart with My song.

READ ON YOUR OWN

Jeremiah 31:25; Philippians 2:15

Don't Divide Up Your Life

*Trust in the L*ORD *and do good.*
—Psalm 37:3

I want you to learn to trust Me in all things. Not just the big things, and not just the things you know you need help with. *All* things.

Don't divide up your life into what you can do by yourself and what you need My help with. Don't say to yourself, "I've got my weekend figured out, but I'll let Jesus figure out my life." Or, "I can handle this argument with my friend, but I need Jesus' help with this big trouble at home."

Train your mind to constantly seek My help and My way—in every situation. Even when you are sure you know the right thing to do, double-check with Me. The more you trust Me, the more you will be able to enjoy life and face each day with confidence.

READ ON YOUR OWN

Psalm 37:4–6; Philippians 4:19

The One Thing

Whatever is good and perfect comes down to us
from God our Father, who created all the lights in the heavens.
He never changes or casts a shifting shadow.
—James 1:17 (NLT)

Every good thing in your life comes from Me. Your home, your favorite things, the people who love you—they are My gifts to you. And though I have given you many pleasures and many things, not one of them is really necessary. Only one thing is truly necessary—having Me in your life.

Before you knew Me as your Savior, you thought your hopes and dreams could be met by things of this world. But now you know better: *I* am the One who fulfills your dreams. I do want you to enjoy the gifts that I give you. But remember to thank Me—the Giver of all good things. And don't start thinking that you have to have these gifts.

Cling to Me, not My gifts. Trust Me to make you complete. The one thing that you *always* need is the one thing you can never lose—My Presence with you.

READ ON YOUR OWN

Psalm 62:5–8; Revelation 1:8; 1 Peter 2:9

People-Pleasers

*Without faith no one can please God. Anyone who comes
to God must believe that he is real and that he rewards those
who truly want to find him.*
—Hebrews 11:6 (ICB)

Don't be a people-pleaser. People-pleasers let their lives be ruled by what other people think. *I have to wear these clothes so they'll hang out with me. I can't sit with those kids—everyone will think I'm a loser. I don't want to try that stuff, but if I don't, I won't fit in.*

You can end up in scary or even dangerous situations trying to please others. Other people aren't perfect. They don't have perfect judgment, and they don't always want what is best for you. Besides, you can't really know what they truly think of you. So being a people-pleaser is foolish.

Live to please Me instead. Only I am perfect and only I care about you perfectly. Don't look at yourself through the eyes of other people, or treat their opinions as being more important than Mine. See yourself through *My* eyes—and you will see a child of God who is deeply and perfectly loved.

READ ON YOUR OWN

John 4:23–24

The Treasure

The LORD turn his face toward you and give you peace.
—Numbers 6:26

I died a criminal's death to buy you the gift of Peace. But instead of accepting My gift, it sometimes seems that you're ignoring it. You hold on to your worries, fears, and loneliness so tightly that you can't receive My Peace. It hurts Me to see you all tied up in anxious knots. This is not what I want for you.

You feel you are too busy and stressed to bring your problems to Me. But here's the truth: The busier and more stressed you are, the more you need to spend time with Me. Take a deep breath, and then take another one—and another. Be still in My Presence. Let My Peace grow inside you as you trust Me with all your worries. Hold on to My gift of Peace like the treasure that it is.

READ ON YOUR OWN

Psalm 46:10; Numbers 6:25

Tough It Out

You know that you learn to endure by having your faith tested.
—James 1:3 (CEV)

"Tough it out." "Stay strong." "Endure." You hear these words a lot when people are talking about sports. But they don't sound so great when you're talking about your life. And yet, that is what you must do: Tough it out, stay strong, and endure.

It's just a fact. You are going to have troubles in this life. The devil is your enemy. So he is going to throw everything he has at you. Problems at school, home, and with friends. Fear, loneliness, and doubt. Expect these troubles, and stand strong. And when the evil one attacks, give thanks.

Yes, give thanks! Thank Me for being able to bring good out of everything. Praise Me for the chance to see My Power in your life. Worship Me—the God who always has a purpose, and who will not let the evil one snatch you away. And thank Me for the spiritual strength you gain by enduring your troubles bravely.

READ ON YOUR OWN

James 1:2–4; Psalm 107:21–22

Powerful Protection

Let us look only to Jesus. He is the one who began our faith,
and he makes our faith perfect.
—Hebrews 12:2 (ICB)

As you go step by step through this day, remind yourself often that *I am with you.* This promise of My Presence is a powerful protection.

Your life is like traveling down a road. As you go down it, you will encounter potholes and ditches all along the way. Many voices—some of them "friendly"—will call to you, trying to get your attention, and tempting you away from the right road. But don't listen to them. Don't even look at them. If you take your eyes off Me and follow another's path, you are in serious danger. Just a few steps away from your true path are pits of self-pity and discouragement, as well as traps of pride and rebellion.

The only way to stay on the right road is to keep your focus on Me. Trusting in My Presence is your best protection.

READ ON YOUR OWN

Matthew 28:20; Hebrews 12:1

I Am Your Comfort

The Father is a merciful God, who always gives us comfort.
He comforts us when we are in trouble, so that we can share
that same comfort with others in trouble.
—2 Corinthians 1:3–4 (CEV)

This world is tough. Some days your spirit can really take a beating. Some days you just need to be comforted.

Because I am always with you, it takes only the slightest glance in My direction—the softest whisper—to connect you with Me and My comfort. I wrap you up in My arms so that you are protected from the kicks and punches of this world.

I comfort you, and then I bless you with the ability to comfort others. You see, I am the God who can bring good out of all things. Out of your hurts, I give you understanding—an understanding of how others are hurting—and an ability to comfort them.

READ ON YOUR OWN

Psalm 34:4–6; Psalm 105:4

You Are Valuable

Consider the ravens: They do not sow or reap,
they have no storeroom or barn; yet God feeds them.
And how much more valuable you are than birds!
—Luke 12:24

Worry is the result of imagining a future without Me in it. So your best defense against worry is to stay in contact with Me—both talking to Me and listening to Me.

Sometimes you do have to think about the future. The key is *how* you think about it. If you only think about the things *you* must do to plan and be prepared, then you will start to worry.

So when you must plan ahead, follow these two rules: First, don't spend very much time thinking about the future. The more you think about it, the easier it is to start worrying. And second, always include Me in your thoughts. Don't just imagine what you will do—imagine what *I* will do.

You can trust Me to take care of you—today *and* in the future. Remember how very valuable you are to Me!

READ ON YOUR OWN
Luke 12:22–23, 25–26; Ephesians 3:20–21

The Good Shepherd

I am the good shepherd; I know my sheep and my sheep know me—
just as the Father knows me and I know the Father—and I lay down
my life for the sheep.
—John 10:14–15

The shepherd has a very important job. It is up to him to guide his sheep. He leads them to food and water and places to rest. He guides them away from dangerous cliffs. He protects them from wild animals that want to hurt them. And a good shepherd will even die to protect his sheep. Sheep cannot survive without a shepherd.

That is what I am—your Shepherd. I lead you to places in My Word that feed your hungry soul. I give you the Living Water of My Presence. I guide you away from temptations and sins. I protect you from the evil one who wants to hurt you. And I have already died for you.

I am not just a good shepherd—I am *the* Good Shepherd. Follow Me as I guide you through this day.

READ ON YOUR OWN

Isaiah 26:7

October 19

Be Real

*Keep putting into practice all you learned and received from me—
everything you heard from me and saw me doing. Then the God of
peace will be with you.*
—Philippians 4:9 (NLT)

It saddens Me to watch My children build up walls between
themselves and the people around them. They pretend they
don't have the same struggles and problems as everyone else.

It even happens at church. You put on your Sunday clothes and
your Sunday smiles. Then you tell everyone you are just fine,
while inside you are full of fear and worry and loneliness. But
you don't dare to say that because—*What would people think*?

The best way to tear down these walls is to focus on My Presence
with you. Talk to Me, worship Me, delight in Me—and you will
feel safe enough to be *real* with others. When your main focus is
on Me, you can stop worrying about what people think. Then you
will be able to smile at others with My Joy and love them with
My Love.

READ ON YOUR OWN

1 John 1:5–7; Exodus 33:14; Philippians 4:8

My Wonderful Works

I praise you because I am fearfully and wonderfully made;
your works are wonderful.
—Psalm 139:14

I carefully crafted every detail of the human body—the way the mind thinks, the way the heart pumps blood to the body, and the way the nerves and senses all work together. I created everything just the way I wanted it. And then I said, "It is very good!"

I created *you* just the way I wanted you. The shade of your hair, the shape of your eyes, the crook of your grin, the slant of your nose—all good. Yet looking in the mirror of this world, you may think you don't measure up.

You look at pictures of movie stars and magazine models—pictures created by computer imaging, not by Me—and you feel like they're better than you. Look at *Me* instead. Look in the mirror of My Love.

As My Life flows into you, you become more and more attractive, on the inside most of all. *My works are wonderful*—especially you!

READ ON YOUR OWN

Colossians 1:29; 1 John 1:7

Tell It to Me

The Lord gave me what I had, and the Lord has taken it away.
Praise the name of the Lord!
—Job 1:21 (NLT)

You don't like it when your plans are messed with. You planned to go to the movies, but your parents said no. You wanted to spend the summer goofing off, but you ended up babysitting instead. You had a goal in mind, but I said, "Not now."

When you don't get to do what you want, you feel like stomping your foot and yelling, "No!" But instead, you push your anger and frustration down inside you. I want you to let that frustration out—to Me. I'll understand, and I'll help you sort through it. Then—and this is the really tough part—praise Me.

Remember that all good things—your possessions, your family and friends, your health and talents, even your time—are *gifts* from Me. Thank Me for the good things I give you, but do not cling to them. Be willing to let go of anything I take from you, including your plans. But don't ever let go of My hand!

READ ON YOUR OWN

Psalm 139:23–24; 1 Peter 5:6

Joy in Your Hardest Day

. . . look for it as for silver and search for it as for hidden treasure.
—Proverbs 2:4

Adventurers in movies, real-life archaeologists, even kids love to spend time looking for lost or hidden treasure. They hope to find gold, silver, jewels, or other valuable things. But as wonderful as those treasures are, they don't compare to the Joy of this day and My Presence with you.

Some days, you don't have to search for Joy at all; it's just there, everywhere you look. Other days, you can't seem to find it, even though you're digging deep. Instead of buried treasure, all you're turning up is dull, gray rocks.

That's when I want you to remember that I have created this day, and that I am with you—whether you sense My Presence or not. Start talking with Me about whatever is on your mind. Be glad that I understand you perfectly—that I know exactly what you're going through. Keep talking with Me, and you'll start to feel better—and better. Just being in My Company can bring Joy into your hardest day.

READ ON YOUR OWN

Psalm 21:6

Do You Feel It?

You have shown me the path to life, and you make me glad by being near to me. Sitting at your right side, I will always be joyful.
—Psalm 16:11 (CEV)

As you decide to come close to Me, the Light of My Presence shines brightly upon you. Do you feel it? It's that warm feeling when you know you've done something that makes Me smile. It's that Peace in your heart when you've poured out all your sorrows to Me. It's that bubbling-over Joy that fills your voice when you sing My praises. It's that perfect Love I always have for you—even when you mess up.

This is one of those wonderful things about Me—the closer you get to Me, the closer I draw you to Me . . . which brings Me closer to you . . . and on and on and on.

Do you feel that Joy? Open your heart to Me—and receive even *more* joy!

READ ON YOUR OWN

John 17:20–23; Psalm 16:11

Wired

By the seventh day God had finished the work he had been doing;
so on the seventh day he rested from all his work.
—Genesis 2:2

Television, cell phones, the Internet—this electronic age keeps you "wired" much of the time. When you're an electrical appliance, being wired is a good thing. But when you are human, being wired can be exhausting. It also makes it harder for you to find Me in your moments.

I created you to need rest. At creation, I even gave you the example of rest by taking a break from all My work. But the world has gotten so twisted that it makes you feel guilty about taking time to rest. This is a trick of the devil. If he can keep you "wired" most of the time—too busy to even stop and look for Me—then he wins.

Tell the devil to get lost. Then lie down, close your eyes, and whisper, "Jesus, help me rest." I'll cover you with a blanket of Peace and watch over you as you rest in Me.

READ ON YOUR OWN

Psalm 23:1–3; Genesis 2:3; Luke 1:79

Who I Am

She will give birth to a son, and you are to give him the name Jesus,
because he will save his people from their sins.
—Matthew 1:21

I am *God with you*. You hear about this so often in church. But don't ever let it become ordinary. Don't ever stop living in awe of Me.

Stop and think for a moment about who I am. My Name is Jesus. It means "the Lord saves." I save you. I save you from the troubles and despair of this world. And I save you from your sins for all eternity.

I am also Immanuel, which means "God with us." *God with you.* I am always with you, and I'm always waiting to hear from you. Tell me about whatever makes you happy, whatever upsets you, whatever is on your mind.

Don't ever get so used to Me that you forget the wonder of who I am or the Joy of knowing Me—the God and Creator of all the universe.

READ ON YOUR OWN

Matthew 1:23; Acts 2:28

Let Me Be Your Everything

I am the vine, and you are the branches.
If a person remains in me and I remain in him, then he produces
much fruit. But without me he can do nothing.
—John 15:5 (ICB)

Come to Me when you're hurting, and I will soothe your pain. Come to Me when you're filled with Joy, and I will multiply it many times over. I am everything you need, just when you need it.

Television personalities, books, and magazines tell you to watch this or read this, and all your problems will be fixed. *You can do it!* they say. *Be confident! Be strong! Do it all on your own! Put yourself first!* But all of this is a trick by the evil one to keep you away from Me. If he can keep you from drawing on My Power, he wins—and you lose.

I have called you to live differently from the world—to depend on Me to meet all your needs. That's where you'll find true confidence and strength.

Let Me be your everything. I am all you need.

READ ON YOUR OWN

Philippians 4:19; James 1:4

It All Starts with Me

In the beginning God created the heavens and the earth.
—Genesis 1:1

I t all starts with Me—the universe, the earth, your life. And now I want your day to start with Me.

Look around at all the things I have created. The thousands of different animals and birds. The millions of different flowers and trees. A new sunset every day for thousands of years. I am the most creative Being imaginable. And I want to pour some of that same creativity into your life.

Many people get so caught up in their own plans for the future that they don't see the choices they need to make each day. They just sleepwalk through their days, following the same old boring paths. But if you live close to Me, I will lead you along fresh trails of adventure—showing you new, exciting things.

Don't worry about what's on the road up ahead—or which way you should go. When you get to a choice-point, I will help you choose the right way. Stay close to Me, and I will guide you step by step.

READ ON YOUR OWN

Psalm 32:8

That's Not Fair

If someone does wrong to you, then forgive him.
Forgive each other because the Lord forgave you.
—Colossians 3:13 (ICB)

ife is not fair. You hear that a lot, but it can still be hard to accept. People will say and do things that hurt your feelings, things you don't deserve. But when someone mistreats you, try to see it as a chance to show them My grace and to grow in your own faith.

Don't try to get even. See how quickly you can forgive. And don't tell everyone around you what happened. Just let it go. Don't worry about what others think—*My* opinion is the one that really counts.

When others mistreat you, remember this: I freely forgive all your sins. I clothe you in shining robes of righteousness bought with My own blood. This isn't fair either—it is the amazing gift of My grace.

When others treat you unfairly, remember that My ways with you are *much* better than fair. My ways are Peace and Love—poured out into your heart by My Spirit.

READ ON YOUR OWN

Isaiah 61:10; Ephesians 1:7–8; Romans 5:5

Stay with Me

For we are God's masterpiece. He has created us anew in Christ Jesus, so we can do the good things he planned for us long ago.
—Ephesians 2:10 (NLT)

Spend some more time with Me. I know today is a busy day and you have much to do, but stay with Me for a few more minutes. I want to enjoy your company. I also want to prepare you for this day.

Great athletes take time to think carefully about what is ahead—going through it in their minds before they move their bodies. In the same way, sitting quietly in My Presence prepares you for the day ahead—for the good things I planned for you.

Only *I* know what will happen today. If you don't let Me prepare you, you may get tired and feel like giving up. Rest a moment with Me—and then we'll have a great day *together*.

READ ON YOUR OWN

Hebrews 12:3

The Bells of Heaven

I am the good shepherd. . . . My sheep know my voice,
and I know them.
—John 10:14, 27 (CEV)

I am with you. I am with you. I am with you.

The bells of heaven continually ring out this promise. Some people never hear it, because they are so busy listening to the noise of this world. Others hear it only once or twice in their whole lives—in rare moments when they seek Me first. But I want My sheep—My children—to hear My promise all the time, because I am their ever-present Shepherd.

To hear Me, you must be still and quiet. Go to your room, outside to a favorite swing, or anywhere you can be quiet and still. And then listen as I speak to your heart.

The more you practice stillness, the easier it becomes. Little by little, you'll learn to carry that stillness with you everywhere. When you go out into the noisy world, listen carefully so you can hear those glorious bells: *I am with you. I am with you. I am with you.*

READ ON YOUR OWN

Jeremiah 29:12–13; John 10:28

While You Listen

"If a person believes in me, rivers of living water
will flow out from his heart. This is what the Scripture says."
Jesus was talking about the Holy Spirit.
—John 7:38–39 (ICB)

L earn to listen to Me even while you are listening to others. When a friend trusts you enough to pour out heart, soul, and troubles to you, you are standing on holy ground. And you have a holy opportunity to help. But if you use only your own thoughts and wisdom to help that person, then what you are offering is only dry crumbs.

Instead, call on the Holy Spirit living inside you. Ask Him to think through you, live through you, love through you. Ask Him for the words to say.

The Spirit fills you with streams of living water—My Love, Joy, and Peace. When you let Him control your listening and speaking, that living water flows through you to others. So listen to Me while you're listening to others. You'll be a blessing to them—and you will be blessed too.

READ ON YOUR OWN

Exodus 3:5; 1 Corinthians 6:19

NOVEMBER

My God will use his wonderful
riches in Christ Jesus to give
you everything you need.

—Philippians 4:19 (ICB)

Cheering You On

Who can accuse the people that God has chosen?
No one! God is the One who makes them right.
—Romans 8:33 (ICB)

In your heart, you want to live in My Presence all the time. But in this world, that can be a very difficult thing to do.

Don't be discouraged if your mind wanders away from Me. And don't accuse yourself of being a failure. Try to see yourself as I see you. I am thrilled by your deep desire to stay close to Me. And I am pleased every time you reach out to talk with Me. Also, I notice the progress you have made since you started trying to live in My Presence.

When you realize your mind has wandered, don't be upset or surprised. This world—and its ruler, the evil one—does everything it can to distract you. So when you force your way through all those distractions to talk to Me, you score a victory. Treasure these victories, and let them encourage you to keep trying. I am cheering you on!

READ ON YOUR OWN

Romans 8:34; Hebrews 4:14–16

That Helpless Feeling

You are kind, Lord, so good and merciful.
You protect ordinary people, and when I was helpless, you saved me
and treated me so kindly that I don't need to worry anymore.
—Psalm 116:5–7 (CEV)

The world tells you that feeling helpless is a bad thing. But *I* tell you it is okay to feel helpless. It doesn't make Me want to avoid you; it makes Me want to take care of you even more—and supply you with more of My Power.

Don't beat yourself up because you need help. Instead, come to Me with all your neediness. I welcome you and your needs, and the Light of My Love will comfort you. Just give your heart to Me. Let Me fill it up with trust.

If your heart is full of trust, you won't whine or rebel when the going gets rough. Instead, you will gather up enough courage to thank Me—even during hard times. This is the kind of trust that pleases Me. And I will reward you with My Strength.

READ ON YOUR OWN

Ephesians 5:20; Isaiah 30:15

Count It as Garbage

Nothing is as wonderful as knowing Christ Jesus my Lord.
I have given up everything else and count it all as garbage.
All I want is Christ.
—Philippians 3:8 (CEV)

When your plans are messed up, talk to Me about it. Talking with Me blesses you and strengthens our friendship. Also, I take the sting out of your disappointment by making something good come of it. So you can be joyful, even when things are going wrong. But it takes practice.

Start by bringing Me small things—the bad grade, the rained-out game. Even small disappointments can focus your thoughts on yourself instead of Me. But when you talk with Me, you see that the things you've lost are nothing compared to the wonders of knowing Me.

You'll need a lot of practice before you can trust Me with big disappointments. But if you keep at it, someday even the greatest things of this world will seem like garbage compared to the Joy of knowing Me—your Savior, Lord, and Friend.

READ ON YOUR OWN

Colossians 4:2; Philippians 3:7

Challenges Are Actually Chances

The LORD gives his people strength.
The LORD blesses them with peace.
—Psalm 29:11 (NLT)

Walk peacefully with Me through this day. You are wondering how you will handle all the things you need to do. But there's really only one way to go through this day—or any day: one step at a time.

I see you rehearsing how you will do this or that—as if you were getting ready for a play. Don't waste time rehearsing; turn to Me instead. Ask Me to guide you, and I will.

One of the greatest things about walking with Me is that the tougher your day is, the more of My Power you can see. The harder things get, the more I help. See your challenges as chances—chances to depend on Me more than usual.

When you don't know what to do, wait for Me. You can be sure that *I* know what I'm doing. So be ready to follow My lead. As we face this day together, I will give strength to you and bless you with My Peace.

READ ON YOUR OWN

Exodus 33:14; Deuteronomy 33:25; Hebrews 13:20–21

My Precious Promises

*I have learned the secret of being happy at any time
in everything that happens.*
—Philippians 4:12 (ICB)

Most people feel happy when things are going right for them. And they feel sad or frustrated when things are not going so well. They believe their happiness depends on what is happening around them at the time. That's why they try so hard to keep everything under their control.

But it is possible to be content with your life no matter what is happening around you.

Don't let your happiness depend on what's going on in your life. Connect your joy to My precious promises: *I am with you and will watch over you wherever you go. I will meet all your needs according to My glorious riches. Nothing in all creation will be able to separate you from My Love.*

READ ON YOUR OWN

Genesis 28:15; Philippians 4:19; Romans 8:38–39

Choices, Choices

The One who sent me is with me.
I always do what is pleasing to him. So he has not left me alone.
—John 8:29 (ICB)

Try to please Me *first*. Before yourself. Before others.

As you go through your day, you will have lots of choices to make. Most of them will be small, everyday choices that you have to make quickly—what to wear, who to sit with at lunch, what to do your book report on.

Many people make their choices out of habit—they choose to do the same things they always do. Or they choose things that please themselves or others. This is not what I want from you. Choose to please Me—in your big decisions and in the small ones too.

When your greatest desire is to please Me, making the right choices becomes easier. A quick, one-word prayer—"*Jesus*"—is all it takes to call upon My help and guidance. Seek to please Me in everything you do.

READ ON YOUR OWN

Hebrews 11:5–6; Psalm 37:4

Reflecting Me

I ask only one thing from the Lord. This is what I want:
Let me live in the Lord's house all my life. Let me see the Lord's
beauty. Let me look around in his Temple.
—Psalm 27:4 (ICB)

See My beauty all around you: in nature, in true friendship, in love. I am the great Artist and all true beauty is a reflection of Me.

I am working to make you more and more beautiful. Bit by bit, I'm clearing out the clutter inside you—the clutter of stuff, of selfishness, of the world. This makes room for My Spirit to take charge of your life. Help Me in this work by letting go of anything I choose to take away. Whether I leave you with a lot or a little, just trust Me. I know what you truly need. And I promise to give you that—abundantly!

READ ON YOUR OWN

Psalm 29:2

In Hard Times

By his power we live and move and exist.
—Acts 17:28 (ICB)

Learn to appreciate hard times. I know that's not easy to do. But as we face troubles and challenges together, your trust in Me will grow.

When you're facing a tough time, think about these three things: your relationship with Me, My promises in the Bible, and past experiences of making it through hard times. Remember that you and I *together* can handle anything.

When you think about the other times I helped you, you may be tempted to say, "That was then; things are different now!" But remember who I am! Your situation may have changed, but I never do. I stay the same throughout time and eternity. Take this truth to heart, and let it inspire your confidence in Me. You live in Me. You walk in Me. You are in Me.

READ ON YOUR OWN

Isaiah 41:10; Psalm 102:27

November 9

I'll Be with You Then

Then Jesus said to his disciples:
"Therefore I tell you, do not worry about your life,
what you will eat; or about your body, what you will wear."
—Luke 12:22

Sit quietly with Me. Let all your worries and fears bubble up into your mind. In My Presence, those bubbles simply pop and disappear.

But there are some fears that bubble up again and again. Often they are future things that you are worried about. You're thinking about the next day, week, month, year. And you're trying to figure out what you'll do. But you are forgetting to include *Me* in your future. Remember: I am with you at all times—including the future.

When worries about the future attack you, say to yourself, "Jesus will be with me then and there. With His help, I can handle anything!" Then get back to living in the Peace of My Presence—*today*.

READ ON YOUR OWN

Luke 12:22–26; Deuteronomy 31:6; 2 Corinthians 10:5

Every Moment

You will let me be with you forever.
—Psalm 41:12 (ICB)

Focus on Me with all your heart, soul, mind, and strength. I am *with* you—wrapping you up in My Love and Peace. So relax. Rest in Me while I shape your mind and cleanse your heart. I am helping you grow into the person I created you to be.

As you go through your day, keep Me in your thoughts. I don't want to be involved in just *part* of your day—I want to be involved in your *whole* day. If something is troubling you, talk to Me about it. If you are bored, fill your time with prayer and praise. If someone gets on your nerves, don't focus on that person. Turn your thoughts back to Me.

Every moment is precious if you keep your attention on Me. And any day can be a good day because My Presence fills all time.

READ ON YOUR OWN

Psalm 89:15–16; 1 John 3:19–20; Jude 24–25

Measuring Your Day

I pray that you will know that the blessings God has promised his holy people are rich and glorious. And you will know that God's power is very great for us who believe.
—Ephesians 1:18–19 (ICB)

W hen you wake up in the morning, your first thoughts are about the day ahead. You think of the things you need to do—and you wonder if you are up to it.

Next time, instead of measuring your day against what you think *you* can do, measure it against what you know *I* can do—which is anything! There is no such thing as a day too tough for Me—not a test day, not a moving day, not a my-parents-had-a-terrible-fight day.

I already know everything you'll face today. And I'll help you face it. I don't give you the same amount of strength every day. When you need more—and when you trust Me more—then I give you more. Look to Me for all that you need. I promise I won't let you down!

READ ON YOUR OWN

Ephesians 1:20; Psalm 105:4; Deuteronomy 33:25

You Can't Earn My Blessings

My cup overflows with blessings.
—Psalm 23:5 (NLT)

This is a time of plenty in your life. Your cup overflows with blessings. Enjoy this time—it is My gift to you.

Don't feel guilty when everything is going well. Don't turn away from My blessings because you think you don't deserve to be so blessed. That is nonsense. The truth is that no one deserves anything from Me. My kingdom is not about earning blessings. And life with Me is not some sort of game in which you earn points to buy prizes. Good behavior doesn't buy blessings.

Instead of trying to work for My blessings, I want you to receive them thankfully. I give you good gifts because I love to see your joy when you receive them. So open your hands and your heart, and accept My blessings gratefully. This brings Joy to you *and* to Me!

READ ON YOUR OWN

John 3:16; Luke 11:9–10; Romans 8:32

Enjoy the Mysteries

*I pray that God, who gives hope, will bless you with complete
happiness and peace because of your faith. And may the power
of the Holy Spirit fill you with hope.*
—Romans 15:13 (CEV)

With Me, some things are a mystery: I am the One who walks
beside you, holding your hand—*and* I am the One who lives
in you to comfort and guide you. I am able to be *both*, all at the
same time.

Here's another mystery: Not only am I in you, but you are also
in Me. We are woven together like the threads of a cloth. There
is nothing in heaven or on earth that can separate you from Me!

As you think about these amazing mysteries, be happy that you
have a God who loves you so very much. Let the knowledge of
My Presence in you and around you fill you up with My Joy and
Peace. These are mysteries that you can't understand—but you
can enjoy them!

READ ON YOUR OWN

Colossians 1:27; Isaiah 42:6; Nehemiah 8:10

The Way *I* See You

Christ had no sin. But God made him become sin.
God did this for us so that in Christ we could become right with God.
—2 Corinthians 5:21 (ICB)

I understand you completely and love you unconditionally. Let these facts soak into your soul. Let them warm your heart and soothe away the bumps and bruises this world has given you.

Dare to see yourself the way *I* see you: shining in the light of My righteousness, washed completely clean by My blood. I see you as the one I created you to be—the one you will really be when heaven becomes your home.

I have given you the gift of My Spirit, who lives inside you. Be grateful. He is there to guide you, strengthen you, and comfort you. Call on Him whenever you need help or guidance. Little by little, as you cooperate with Him, you grow more into the person I created you to be.

READ ON YOUR OWN

Psalm 34:5; 2 Corinthians 3:18; Galatians 5:25

A Better Way

In this world you will have trouble.
But be brave! I have defeated the world!
—John 16:33 (ICB)

You tend to approach problems as if you were going into battle. The problem becomes the focus of your thoughts. Your mind and body tense up as you prepare to fight. It's the ultimate battle: "You versus The Problem." And if you don't win a total victory right away, you feel defeated.

There is a better way. It doesn't have to be a winner-takes-all fight. When a problem starts to take over your thoughts, talk to Me about it. Step back and get some space between you and your trouble. Let Me show you things from My point of view. You'll probably find that it's not really such a big deal.

There will always be trouble to face in this world. But what matters is that you always have *Me* on your side. When you remember that I'm the all-time Champion who defeated the world, big things get cut down to their real size. You'll be able to see that your problems aren't so serious after all.

READ ON YOUR OWN

Psalm 89:15

The Navigator

You guide me with your counsel, leading me to a glorious destiny.
—Psalm 73:24 (NLT)

As you think about the day that's ahead, it's not looking like a straight, smooth path. You see a maze instead, full of crazy twists and turns, with lots of choices to make. How are you going to navigate your way down that path? But you forget one thing—you're not the navigator, *I* am.

Every trip needs a navigator. Let Me be yours. Remember, I promised to never leave you and to always guide you.

As you let Me take the lead, look again at your path. You'll notice that a peaceful fog has settled over it. You can see only a few steps in front of you. That fog is My protection, to keep you from worrying about the future. It also helps you keep your thoughts on Me—in the here and now. So relax, and let Me be your Guide. I'm holding you by your right hand.

READ ON YOUR OWN

Psalm 73:23; 1 Corinthians 13:12

My Voice

*Whether you turn to the right or to the left, your ears will hear
a voice behind you, saying, "This is the way; walk in it."*
—Isaiah 30:21

Listen to My Voice and follow Me. It sounds simple, but it is not always easy. There are lots of different voices, and they are all saying, "Follow me! This is the way for you to go!"

If you listen to the world, it will lead you down a path filled with glitter, glamour, and fun—at first. But all too soon the glitter, glamour, and fun will run out, and you will be all alone.

Even some Christian voices can confuse you, saying, "Sing this song, not that one!" "Pray this way, not that way!" Like the Pharisees of the Bible, they make up rules that I never wanted. But I died to set you free from man-made rules.

How do you know which voice is Mine? Spend time with Me—quiet time in prayer and praise. Just as good friends know each other's voices, you will come to know Mine. And I will tell you the right way to go.

READ ON YOUR OWN

Romans 8:1–2; John 10:27; Psalm 23:1–3

Words of Grace

Do not worry about anything.
But pray and ask God for everything you need.
—Philippians 4:6 (ICB)

Come to Me and rest. Stop trying to figure everything out. Instead, trust in the One who already knows *everything*. Let My Peace soak into your heart until you feel complete. This is how I designed you to live—close to Me.

When you're around others—family, friends, classmates—you often get too focused on what you think they expect from you. You get worn out trying to give them what they want—to win their approval. When you do this, you offer them dry crumbs instead of the *living water* of My Spirit.

This is not the way I want you to live! Try to stay in touch with Me even during your busiest times. Then you will live in My Peace, and My Spirit will give you words of grace—to bless others.

READ ON YOUR OWN

Philippians 4:6–7; John 7:38; Ephesians 5:18–20

No Matter Where I Lead

You keep your loving promise. You lead the people you have saved.
With your strength you will guide them to your holy land.
—Exodus 15:13 (ICB)

Follow Me. No matter where I lead you, just follow Me. Don't worry about how everything will turn out. Just trust Me, and I'll show you the way.

Think of your life as an adventure, with Me as your Guide and Companion. Don't worry about where our path will lead tomorrow—just live in the adventure of *today*. Keep your mind on staying close to Me.

If our path takes us to the bottom of a steep cliff, don't be afraid. Just hold tightly to My hand, and take a deep breath. I'll help you climb all the way up to the top. And when we come to a peaceful resting place, stop there a while and rest with Me.

You already know where our journey will end. Someday I will take you into heaven—to live with Me there forever. But for now, just follow Me as I guide you along today's path. And enjoy the adventures you share with Me—your faithful Guide.

READ ON YOUR OWN

Psalm 27:13–14

Making the Grade

For it is by grace you have been saved,
through faith—and this not from yourselves, it is the gift of God—
not by works, so that no one can boast.
—Ephesians 2:8–9

There are so many things you get graded on. There are report cards for school and points for sports. There are scores for talent shows and beauty contests. And in a few years, you'll even be tested on your driving. Almost everywhere you go, you are graded on how well you perform.

But I don't keep score. Not ever. And I don't grade you on your performance. There is no heavenly grade book that says: Prayer Time—B, Kindness—A-, Patience—C+.

So change your focus from your performance to My loving Presence. The Light of My Love shines on you always—no matter how well you're doing or how you feel. You don't need to worry about making the grade. Because you are My child, it's A+ all the way!

READ ON YOUR OWN

Ephesians 3:16–19; Psalm 62:8

The Best Gifts Ever

Jesus himself stood among them and said to them,
"Peace be with you."
—Luke 24:36

Think about the best gift you've ever gotten: that new computer, the cool video game, the bike you kept seeing in the store. They're all nice gifts.

But I have much better gifts for you. Gifts of supernatural proportions! They are My Presence and My Peace. These gifts never get holes in them. They never need new batteries. And they never go out of style.

They also can't be purchased at the local store or off the Internet. There is only one way to get these gifts. And that is to come to Me with a thankful, trusting heart.

I created you to glorify Me. This means you can never spend too much time praising and thanking Me. Praising Me says you know that I am God and you trust My control over your life. Thanking Me opens your heart to receive My Presence and My Peace—the richest, most awesome gifts of all.

READ ON YOUR OWN

Matthew 28:20; Hebrews 13:15

Windows of Heaven

I will rejoice in the LORD, I will be joyful in God my Savior.
—Habakkuk 3:18

When you come to Me with a thankful heart, it opens up windows of heaven. Spiritual blessings fall freely through those windows and down into your life. A thankful heart opens you up to these blessings, and then you have even *more* reasons to be grateful.

Being thankful brings you many blessings, but it is not a magic formula. Thankful words are really just the language of Love, and they help you grow closer to Me. When you thank Me, it makes a love-connection between your heart and Mine. Just as a telephone connection lets you talk to another person, a loving, thankful heart helps you talk to Me—and Me to you.

Being thankful doesn't mean you close your eyes to the many problems in this world. It means you find Joy in Me—your Savior—in the midst of a messed-up world. I am your hiding place and your strength. And I'm always ready to help you!

READ ON YOUR OWN

Habakkuk 3:17–18; Psalm 46:1

A Bouquet of Treasures

I will lie down and sleep in peace, for you alone,
O LORD, make me dwell in safety.
—Psalm 4:8

As you go through this day, look for the tiny treasures I have placed along your way. I lovingly go before you and plant little pleasures to brighten up your day.

Sometimes these treasures are a part of My creation—a bird hopping by, a multicolored sunset, a tiny wildflower. Other times I use people in your life to deliver My pleasures to you—an encouraging note from a teacher, a hug from a friend at just the right moment, a smile from someone you don't even know.

Collect these treasures one by one. When you reach the end of your day, you will have gathered a beautiful bouquet of them. Offer them back to Me with a thankful heart. Then receive My Peace as you lie down in your bed, letting your thankful thoughts sing you to sleep.

READ ON YOUR OWN

Romans 8:38–39; Psalm 4:7

Flipping the Switch

*Give thanks to the L*ORD*, for he is good; his love endures forever.*
—Psalm 118:1

W hen you thank Me for the difficult things in your life, suddenly they are no longer as difficult. How this works is a mystery.

But if you will give Me thanks—even for the things that make you sad or upset—then I will give you Joy. And you can have that Joy no matter what is happening.

For those who don't know Me well, thanking Me for heartaches and hardships seems impossible—even silly. But if you step out in faith and thank Me, you will be blessed. You may still be in the same yucky situation, but it will be as if someone flipped on the light switch in a dark room. You'll see things in the Light of My Presence—from *My* point of view—and realize that you aren't alone. My Presence will make your troubles not so troublesome.

READ ON YOUR OWN

Ephesians 5:20; Psalm 89:15

Never Stop Praying

Always be joyful. Never stop praying.
Be thankful in all circumstances.
—1 Thessalonians 5:16–18 (NLT)

Never stop praying. How is that even possible? Try thanking Me for every blessing you encounter in your day. Not just your meals, or when you aced your test—but when you wake up, when you finish a class, when you get to see your friends, even when you face the "hidden blessings" of troubles or challenges.

If you are serious about learning to pray at all times, then thank Me in every situation. Don't get hung up on saying the "right" words—prayer doesn't have to be fancy or formal. Just say, "Thank You" and mean it. This is a great starting point for all your other prayers too.

When you're caught up in thanking Me, you won't have time for worrying or complaining. This will make you much happier. You will be training your mind to keep talking with Me. And that's really what "never stop praying" is all about.

READ ON YOUR OWN

James 4:8; Romans 15:13

Your Greatest Protection

I will offer you a sacrifice of thanksgiving
*and call on the name of the L*ORD.
—Psalm 116:17 (NLT)

If you want to have a thankful heart, you must work to protect it. Remember that you live in a fallen world, full of sin. Both blessings and sorrows are all around you, and they are mixed up together. Work to keep your heart and mind focused on the good things.

Too many of My children choose to focus on the hard times and the trouble. They walk through a day filled with beauty and brightness, and they see only the gray of sorrow and sin. They forget to look for My blessings, and darkness fills their minds.

Thankfulness is your greatest protection against that darkness. When your heart is thankful, you know that the Light of My Presence is shining on you. And you can walk through even the grayest day with Joy in your heart.

READ ON YOUR OWN

Psalm 118:24

The Language of Heaven

Come into his city with songs of thanksgiving.
Come into his courtyards with songs of praise.
—Psalm 100:4 (ICB)

When you live your life praising and thanking Me for the blessings I give you each day, your life becomes filled with miracles. It is as if a blindfold has been removed from your eyes. With your eyes wide open, you see more and more of My glorious riches. So let your thankfulness sing out My praises!

A thankful heart keeps you focused on Me and what I am doing in your life. Instead of trying to be in control, you relax and make Me the Center of your life. This is the way I created you to live, and it is a way of Joy.

Your joyful praises are the language of heaven—and the true language of your heart.

READ ON YOUR OWN

Colossians 3:15; Acts 9:18; Revelation 19:3–6; Psalm 100:5

Always and Perfectly

*Let them give thanks to the L*ord *for his unfailing love
and his wonderful deeds for men.*
—Psalm 107:21

T here is nothing—and no one—in this world that is perfect.
Things break, friends let you down, and even your parents
lose their cool sometimes.

Only I am perfect. And I love you perfectly—*always*. Let your
body, mind, and spirit relax in that fact. Be awed by the vastness
of My Love for you. It is wider than any continent, longer than
any road, higher than any mountain, and deeper than any ocean.
This vast Love is yours—forever!

The best possible response to My Love is thankfulness. Thank
Me for loving you, for being your Savior, and for taking care of
you. Then just watch to see how much I bless you.

READ ON YOUR OWN

1 Peter 5:7; Ephesians 3:16–19; Psalm 107:22

November 29

The Key

The Lord will always lead you. He will satisfy your needs in dry lands.
He will give strength to your bones. You will be like a garden that has
much water. You will be like a spring that never runs dry.
—Isaiah 58:11 (ICB)

In this world, it's not easy to admit that you need someone else. It's often seen as a sign of weakness. But that isn't true. I created you with a need—a need for Me. And I've put you in situations that reveal your neediness. So don't view it as a sign of weakness; it's a sign of My divine plan.

Your greatest need is for the Peace you find in My Presence. It's not like the peace of this world, which depends on everything going just right. It's not something you can get for yourself through hard work or sheer willpower. True, lasting Peace comes only from Me. You have to spend time in My Presence to receive it.

Peace comes from trusting Me and My ways in your life—through good times and hard times. This isn't easy, especially during *really* hard times. But be encouraged: Needing Me is the key to knowing Me better. And knowing Me is the greatest gift of all.

READ ON YOUR OWN

Isaiah 40:11

Heavenly Light

Our citizenship is in heaven.
—Philippians 3:20

There are a lot of things in this world that need fixing. There are a lot of things in *your* world that need fixing: broken promises, broken relationships, and much more. But you don't have to be the fix-it person. In fact, you *can't* be. You're only human.

Still, that doesn't stop you from trying. When you see something wrong, you tend to jump right into problem solving. But that is not your main responsibility in life. Your main responsibility is your relationship with Me. If a problem enters your day, talk with Me about it. Ask for My thoughts on it. Rather than just jumping in and trying to fix everything, ask Me to show you what is truly important.

Remember, this world is only temporary, and you are just passing through it. Your true home is in heaven—and even your biggest problems fade in the heavenly Light of eternity.

READ ON YOUR OWN

Psalm 32:8; Luke 10:41–42; Philippians 3:21

DECEMBER

For a child is born to us. . . . And he
will be called: Wonderful Counselor,
Mighty God, Everlasting Father,
Prince of Peace.

—Isaiah 9:6 (NLT)

December 1

Surviving the Storms

I have loved you with an everlasting love.
—Jeremiah 31:3

I love you—*eternally*. Think about the awesome mystery of an eternal Love—a Love that began before you were even born, that continues now, and that will go on until long after your life on this earth is over.

Some people are frightened by the idea of eternity. They don't want to think about death or what happens after it. So they keep themselves busy with nonstop activity and amusement.

But it is only by being still in My Presence that you can experience My everlasting Love. And you need that experience of My Love to survive the storms of life. When things get rough, knowing *about* Me is not enough. You need to really *know Me*—so that you can trust Me to get you through the storm.

So be still and get to know Me better. This will strengthen your friendship with Me—and that is the best protection against sinking during life's storms.

READ ON YOUR OWN

Lamentations 3:22–23, 25–26

Prince of Peace

And he will be called Wonderful Counselor, Mighty God,
Everlasting Father, Prince of Peace.
—Isaiah 9:6

I have many names: Wonderful Counselor, Mighty God, Everlasting Father, Prince of Peace, King of kings, and Lord of lords. But in this messed-up world, it is perhaps as Prince of Peace that you need Me most.

Because I never leave your side, My Peace is always with you. You need this Peace each moment to live out My plan for your life. Sometimes you may want to take shortcuts—to reach your goal as quickly as possible. But if taking the shortcut means you turn your back on My peaceful Presence, then don't do it. Keep walking with Me along paths of Peace—even in this crazy world.

READ ON YOUR OWN

John 20:19–21; Psalm 25:4

December 3

Your Hope and My Promise

For our struggle is not against flesh and blood, but against the rulers, against the authorities, against the powers of this dark world and against the spiritual forces of evil in the heavenly realms.
—Ephesians 6:12

There is nothing that the evil one hates more than your closeness to Me. He will do anything to pull you away. So don't be surprised by his fiery attacks on your mind.

There is a massive spiritual war being fought every day. When you find yourself in the thick of the battle, cry out, "Jesus, help me!" At that very instant, the battle becomes Mine. Your job is simply to trust Me as I fight for you.

When My Name is used in the right way, it has unlimited Power to bless and protect. At the end of time, every knee will bow *at the Name of Jesus*. People who have used My Name as a swear word will tremble in fear. But all those who have used My Name to draw near Me will be filled with glorious Joy. This is your hope—and My promise to you.

READ ON YOUR OWN

1 Samuel 17:47; Philippians 2:9–10; 1 Peter 1:8–9

A Small Sacrifice

Devote yourselves to prayer with an alert mind and a thankful heart.
—Colossians 4:2 (NLT)

My thoughts are not your thoughts, and your ways are not My ways. Just as the heavens are higher than the earth, so are My ways and thoughts higher than yours.

When you come to spend time with Me, remember who I really am. I am the King of kings and Lord of lords! Never stop being amazed at being able to talk with the King of the entire universe—anytime, anyplace.

As you spend time in My Presence, I am training you to think My thoughts. My Spirit goes to work inside you. Sometimes He speaks to you through certain Bible verses. And other times He allows you to hear Me "speak" into your mind. Either way, this training strengthens you and prepares you for whatever you will face.

Take time to listen to My voice. Give Me this small sacrifice of your time, and I will bless you far more than you could ever imagine.

READ ON YOUR OWN

Isaiah 55:8–9; Psalm 116:17

A Prayer I Love to Answer

*When Jacob awoke from his sleep, he thought, "Surely the L*ORD* is in this place, and I was not aware of it."*
—Genesis 28:16

W hen Jacob ran away from his angry brother, Esau, he went to sleep on a stone pillow in a land that seemed empty and gloomy. But he dreamed about heaven and angels and promises of My Presence. And when he awoke, he thought, "Surely the Lord is in this place, and I was not aware of it."

Jacob's discovery was not only for himself, but for everyone who seeks Me. I am everywhere. I am above you, below you, and all around you. There is no place that I am not. So if you find yourself feeling distant from Me, say: "Surely the Lord is in this place!" Then ask Me to open the eyes of your heart so that you can "see" My Presence. This is a prayer I love to answer!

READ ON YOUR OWN

Psalm 31:20; Genesis 28:11–15

What I Want Most

*Love the L*ORD* your God with all your heart
and with all your soul and with all your strength.*
—Deuteronomy 6:5

S taying close to Me is really all about love—My Love for you and your love for Me.

Too many people believe their faith is all about what they *do*. They give Me their time, their money, and their service, but they don't give Me the one thing I want most—their hearts.

Be careful not to let your faith become a set of rules to follow: church on Sunday, read your Bible, pray ten minutes each day. Rules lead to habits—things you do without even thinking—lulling your soul to sleep.

What I search for in My children is an *awakened soul* that finds My Presence thrilling! There is abundant Joy in My Presence—and it is for *you*. After all, I created you to glorify Me and enjoy Me forever. I provide the Joy; your job is to live close to Me. This brings Glory to Me and Joy to you!

READ ON YOUR OWN

Colossians 3:23; Psalm 16:11

Every Detail

And even the very hairs of your head are all numbered.
—Matthew 10:30

I am with you in all that you do. At home, at school, on the playground. When you sleep, when you eat, when you laugh, and when you cry. I know every detail of your life—even the number of hairs on your head. There is nothing that I don't notice.

But your own awareness of Me comes and goes. Sometimes you feel Me right next to you, and you feel safe and whole. Other times the problems of the day fill your mind and you lose sight of Me. Then you feel alone and empty.

Learn to keep your eyes on Me at all times and in all situations. This world is constantly changing, but My Presence is always with you. Fix your eyes on what is unseen—Me. Then the whole world can march by, and you'll still know My Presence right beside you.

READ ON YOUR OWN

Matthew 10:29–31; Hebrews 11:27; 2 Corinthians 4:18

Be Glad You Are Needy

I want them to be encouraged and knit together by strong ties of love.
I want them to have complete confidence that they understand God's
mysterious plan, which is Christ himself.
—Colossians 2:2 (NLT)

Your needs and My riches are a perfect fit—like the pieces of a puzzle that join together to make a beautiful picture.

I never meant for you to "go it alone," to do it all by yourself. I designed you to need Me, not only for your daily bread but also to fill that deep emptiness inside you. I created that emptiness to lead you to Me. It's part of My plan. So don't try to pretend the emptiness doesn't exist. And don't try to fill it with the lesser gods of this world: people, possessions, and power.

Come to Me with all your needs. Let your defenses down and seek My blessings. As you spend time with Me, your emptiness gets filled with My Love, Joy, and Peace. Be glad you are needy—that helps you get filled up with Me.

READ ON YOUR OWN

Philippians 4:19; Colossians 2:2–3

December 9

Out on a Limb

If you serve me, you must go with me.
—John 12:26 (CEV)

B e willing to step out of your comfort zone. Take a risk and go out on a limb with Me. If that is where I am leading you, then out on that limb is the safest place for you to be.

You want to play it safe, avoid all the risks you can. But taking risks is part of living close to Me. Trying to live a risk-free life tells Me that you don't really trust Me. You have to make a choice: Will you keep trying to be safe at all costs? Or will you follow Me with all your heart?

I may ask you to stand up for someone who can't stand up for himself, to say no to a friend, or to tell a stranger about Me. But I'll give you the strength and the courage to do it.

Life with Me is an adventure. If you stick with Me, you'll not only have My protection, but you'll learn to relax and enjoy the adventure. So be willing to follow wherever I lead—even out on a limb.

READ ON YOUR OWN

Psalm 23:4; Psalm 9:10

Safe and Secure

Even there your hand will guide me, your right hand will hold me fast.
—Psalm 139:10

You want to feel safe and secure. You say you trust Me, but in your private thoughts, you are still trying to fix your world so that it is safe and predictable. Not only is this an impossible goal, but it actually makes you *less* safe and secure.

True safety and security are found only in Me—in depending on My Presence. When your world seems unsteady and scary, grab My hand. I will hold tightly to you and keep you safe.

Instead of searching for a problem-free life, be glad that you have troubles. In the darkness of your trouble, you can see the brightness of My Face more clearly. This helps you feel closer to me.

So hold tightly to My hand, confident that today's problems have a purpose. And remember—you have an eternity of trouble-free living just waiting for you in heaven.

READ ON YOUR OWN

Isaiah 41:10; James 1:2

Faith Is Knowing

Now faith is being sure of what we hope for
and certain of what we do not see.
—Hebrews 11:1

Every moment of every day, I am working for your good. So bring Me all your worries and fear. Talk with Me about everything. Let the Light of My Presence chase your shadows away.

Bring Me your hopes and dreams too. Let's work on them together, changing them little by little from wishes to reality.

All this takes time. Don't try to take shortcuts or rush the process. When you work with Me, you must learn to accept My timing. Remember how long Abraham and Sarah waited for a son? But when Isaac finally came, their joy was even greater because of their long wait.

Faith is *knowing* I will keep My promises—believing that things you are hoping for are as real as things you can already see.

READ ON YOUR OWN

Psalm 36:9; Genesis 21:1–7

The Tip of the Iceberg

I know that you can do all things. No plan of yours can be ruined.
—Job 42:2 (ICB)

I am taking care of you. Every detail of your life is under My control. When you give your heart to Me, I make sure that everything in your life works together for good—even the hard stuff.

Some people look at what happens in the world, and they think the universe is ruled by chance. Things just happen, with little or no meaning. But they are looking at the world through eyes that cannot really see.

Your understanding of this world is like the tip of an iceberg. Only a small part of an iceberg can be seen; the rest is hidden under the surface of the water. And hidden under the surface of this world, there are *mysteries* too big for you to understand.

If you could look through My eyes—seeing how everything fits together—you would see how wonderfully I am caring for you. This is why you must live by faith, not by sight—trusting in My mysterious, loving Presence.

READ ON YOUR OWN

Romans 8:28; Job 42:1–3; 1 Peter 5:7; 2 Corinthians 5:7

Time to Be Holy

You surely know that your body is a temple where the Holy Spirit lives.
The Spirit is in you and is a gift from God.
—1 Corinthians 6:19 (CEV)

Take time to be holy. But how? *Holy* doesn't mean being a goody-goody, or thinking you are better than others. Being holy simply means setting yourself apart for sacred use—*My* use.

Spend some quiet moments with Me. Let Me work in your heart and mind. I am re-creating you into the person I designed you to be.

Be sure to set aside enough time for just being with Me. Your closeness to Me will strengthen your faith and fill you with My Peace. It will also prepare you for the many blessings I want to give you.

When you take time to be holy, your heart becomes a clean temple of My Holy Spirit. He is able to do more in and through you than you could ever ask or imagine. So make time for Me. You won't regret it.

READ ON YOUR OWN

2 Thessalonians 1:10; Psalm 27:4; Ephesians 3:20

I Never Change

Jesus Christ never changes!
He is the same yesterday, today, and forever.
—Hebrews 13:8 (CEV)

Your heart and your mind are much like a radio. The kind of music you hear depends on the station you tune in to. When your heart and mind tune in to the world, you hear confusion. Everything is constantly changing—often for no reason. And it can leave you feeling anxious and afraid.

But when you choose to tune in to Me, you hear the beautiful music of My Peace. It soothes away the worries of this world. And it helps you know how safe and secure you are—because you're Mine.

Unlike the world, I *never* change. You can always count on Me. Start your day by tuning in to Me. Listen quietly in My Presence. Then get up and begin your journey through the day, holding tightly to My hand. I will show you which way to go, and I will smooth out the path before you.

READ ON YOUR OWN

Ecclesiastes 1:2; Proverbs 3:6

December 15

Grab Hold of Hope!

So God has given both his promise and his oath.
These two things are unchangeable because it is impossible for God
to lie. Therefore, we who have fled to him for refuge can have great
confidence as we hold to the hope that lies before us.
—Hebrews 6:18 (NLT)

The hope of heaven. Too many of My children don't really understand what this means. When I talk of *hope*, it isn't just wishful thinking. This hope is My promise for all My children.

As soon as I became your Savior, heaven became your final, permanent home. But there are blessings of this hope that you can enjoy right now! Because your true home is heaven, you know that any troubles you face today are only temporary. *The hope of heaven* helps you through your tough times, brightening even the darkest days. It also helps you keep trusting that I am taking care of you—and everything will be all right.

Don't just wish for heaven—grab hold of the hope of heaven! Let its blessing fill your life today.

READ ON YOUR OWN

Romans 8:23–25; Hebrews 6:19–20; Romans 15:13

Listen to Me

Every morning he wakes me. He teaches me to listen like a student.
—Isaiah 50:4 (ICB)

I am always speaking to you, in the depths of your heart. But you must be still so that you can hear My Voice. I speak in the language of Love. My words fill you with Life and Peace, Joy and Hope. I am teaching you to listen to Me—like a student listening to the teacher.

I want to talk with all My children, but many of them are too busy to listen. This world prizes busyness. A lot of people go along with that mind-set, convinced that being still is a waste of time. Then they wonder why I feel so far away.

To live close to Me, you must put Me first. Seek Me before anything else—before chores, before school, before practice, before fun. When you seek Me first, I pour out My Peace and Joy on you. And My Glory shines in your life like the sun.

READ ON YOUR OWN

Revelation 2:4; Isaiah 60:2

A Perfect Day to Trust

God blesses those who are poor and realize their need for him,
for the Kingdom of Heaven is theirs.
—Matthew 5:3 (NLT)

Come to Me with all your needs, with that huge emptiness inside you. Facing that awful emptiness is the first step toward being filled with My Presence.

So be glad on those days when you can barely get out of bed—when you feel sluggish and just not ready to face the world. Yes, be glad! Tell yourself that this is the perfect day to practice trusting and depending on Me.

If you keep depending on Me throughout your day, you will make a wonderful discovery as you crawl into bed at night. You will discover that My Joy and Peace have become your companions. You may not know exactly when they joined you on your journey through the day. But you will feel the benefits of having been in their company.

The perfect ending to a day like this is to sing yourself to sleep with My praises.

READ ON YOUR OWN

2 Corinthians 4:6; Matthew 5:6;
Colossians 2:9–10; Psalm 150:6

Eternal Glory

We have small troubles for a while now, but they are helping us gain an eternal glory. That glory is much greater than the troubles.
—2 Corinthians 4:17 (ICB)

When you have a problem that goes on and on, with no end in sight, see it as a wonderful opportunity. An ongoing problem is like having a tutor who is always by your side. If you are willing, you can learn so much from your trouble.

Ask Me to open your eyes and your heart to all that I am doing through this problem. I may be teaching you patience or persistence. Perhaps I am strengthening your faith or your courage.

Then thank Me for the lessons you are learning. When you can be thankful for a problem, it loses its power to drag you down. In fact, your thankful attitude lifts you up into heavenly places with Me, where you see the situation from My point of view. This lets you see your problem as a small, temporary trouble that is helping you *gain an eternal Glory*—blessings that will never end!

READ ON YOUR OWN

Isaiah 30:20–21

December 19

Clearing the Clutter

Seek the Kingdom of God above all else, and live righteously,
and he will give you everything you need.
—Matthew 6:33 (NLT)

Do not be overwhelmed by the clutter in your life. By "clutter," I'm not just talking about all that stuff under your bed. I'm including all those endless little chores that you need to do sometime, but not necessarily *now*. For instance, you told your friend you would download that song for her. And your bike tires really need airing up.

All those little tasks will eat up as much time as you give them. So, instead of trying to do everything at once, choose the chores that really need to be done today. Then let the rest of them slip to the back of your mind, so that *I* can be in the front of it.

Remember, your real goal in this life is not to check everything off a to-do list. It is to live close to Me. Seek My Face all throughout this day. Let My Presence clear away the clutter in your mind and flood you with My Peace.

READ ON YOUR OWN

Proverbs 16:3

I Did It for You

*The people stood watching, and the rulers even sneered at him.
They said, "He saved others; let him save himself if he is the Christ
of God, the Chosen One."*
—Luke 23:35

When I came to earth, it wasn't to a palace or a rich family. I was born to a peasant girl and a carpenter, in a stable. My Glory was hidden from all but a few people.

At times, some of My Glory would shine out of Me—especially when I began to do miracles. When the sick were healed, when the storms were stilled, and when the demons fled before Me, people saw it . . . briefly.

At the end of My life, I could have used My awesome Power to save Myself. Thousands of angels would have come to rescue Me from being beaten and made fun of and nailed to a cross. But that was not My Father's plan. So I stayed on the cross—for you. I did it so that your sins could be forgiven and heaven could become your home. I did it so that we could be the best of friends. So let your life become a song of praise to Me, showing My Glory to all the world.

READ ON YOUR OWN

John 2:11; Luke 23:36; Psalm 92:1–5

December 21

Traveling

Jesus replied, "Didn't I tell you that if you had faith,
you would see the glory of God?"
—John 11:40 (CEV)

I have a perfect plan for your life. But I don't show it to you all at once. It is like a road that you must travel one step at a time.

Sometimes the road seems blocked, or it opens up so slowly that you feel frustrated. But then, when the time is right, the way before you suddenly clears. All that you have longed for and worked for is given to you freely—as a gift. And that is when you catch a glimpse of My Power and My Glory.

Don't be afraid of your weakness. It's like a stage where My Power and Glory are the actors, putting on amazing shows. Just keep walking along the path I have prepared for you, depending on My Strength to keep you going. Expect to see some miracles—and you will. Not just anyone can see My miracles, but those who live by faith can see them clearly. When you walk by faith—going step by step with Me—you are able to see My Glory.

READ ON YOUR OWN

Psalm 63:2; 2 Corinthians 5:7

Do as the Wise Men Did

When they saw the star, they rejoiced with exceedingly great joy.
And when they had come into the house, they saw the young Child with
Mary His mother, and fell down and worshiped Him.
—Matthew 2:10–11 (NKJV)

Come and sit with Me for a while. I want you to think about who I really am.

I am the only Son of God. I was born completely human and yet I am completely God—all at the same time. This is a mystery that is beyond your understanding. Rather than trying to figure it out, do as the wise men did. They followed a spectacular star, and then they fell down in humble worship when they found Me.

Praise and worship are the best responses to the wonder of who I am. Sing praises to My holy Name. Gaze at Me in silent worship. Look for a "star" of guidance in your own life, and be ready to follow wherever I lead you. I am the Light from heaven that shines upon you—to guide you along the path of Peace.

READ ON YOUR OWN

Luke 1:35; John 1:14; Matthew 2:9; Luke 1:78–79

Both God and Man

Come, let us bow down in worship,
*let us kneel before the L*ORD *our Maker; for he is our God.*
—Psalm 95:6–7

I am the King of kings and Lord of lords. I am also your Shepherd, your Companion, and your Friend—the One who *never* lets go of your hand.

Worship Me in My holy Majesty. Come close to Me, and rest in My Presence. You need Me as both God and Man. Even though I am God, I had to come into this world as a baby and grow into the Man who became your Savior. That's the only way I could meet your biggest need—to be saved from your sins.

Since I was willing to give up all of heaven for you and to die a terrible death for you—then you can be sure I will give you everything you need. So trust Me as your Savior, Lord, and Friend. Rejoice in everything I have done for you, and My Light will shine through you into the world.

READ ON YOUR OWN

1 Timothy 6:15–16; Romans 8:32; 2 Peter 1:19

Celebrate the Gift

*Before the mountains were born, before you gave birth to the earth
and the world, from beginning to end, you are God.*
—Psalm 90:2 (NLT)

I am eternal. Forever. When I speak, it is from the depths of eternity. Before the world was formed, I AM! And when this world is gone, I will still be the same.

I have come to live inside your heart. I am Christ in you. I, your Lord and Savior, am alive within you! Learn to tune in to My living Presence by seeking Me in quietness.

As you celebrate the wonder of My birth in Bethlehem, remember to celebrate also *your* birth into eternal life. This amazing gift was My purpose for coming into your world. Enjoy My gift with a humble, thankful heart. Take time to explore how huge My Love for you really is. And let My Peace rule in your heart, because you know how much I love you.

READ ON YOUR OWN

Colossians 1:27; Colossians 3:15

I Became Poor

You know that Christ was rich, but for you he became poor.
Christ did this so that by his being poor you might become rich.
—2 Corinthians 8:9 (ICB)

Try to imagine what that first, long-ago Christmas was like for Me. Think about how much I gave up when I came to this earth as a baby. I set aside My Glory so that I could be part of the human race. I gave up the Power of heaven to become a helpless infant. I left the majesty and perfection of heaven to be born in a dirty stable. That was a dark night for Me, even though angels lit up the sky announcing "Glory!" to amazed shepherds.

But I did it all for you.

When you sit quietly with Me, you experience the opposite of what I went through. As you focus on Me—and all I gave up for you—heaven opens up just a bit, giving you a glimpse of My Glory. I became poor so that you could become rich. Sing praises to My holy Name!

READ ON YOUR OWN

2 Corinthians 4:6; Philippians 2:6–7; Luke 2:13–14

It Really Is Unconditional

God is love. Whoever lives in love lives in God, and God in him.
—1 John 4:16

Every second of every day, I give you the gift of My unconditional Love. It is truly a gift, with no strings attached.

Many of My children have trouble understanding the "unconditional" part. It means that nothing in heaven or on earth—not even your sins—can cause Me to stop loving you.

When you think you are doing all right, you may feel more loved. And when you mess up, you may feel less loved. But those are only your feelings. My Love is perfect, and that means it never changes.

When you've messed up, you often feel unworthy of My Love. You may pull away from Me without realizing it—and then think *I* have pulled away from you. But the whole time, all I want to do is wrap you up in My arms and surround you with My Love.

No matter how you are feeling, come to Me. My Love really is unconditional.

READ ON YOUR OWN

1 John 4:15–18; Deuteronomy 33:27; Psalm 13:5

December 27

While You Wait

Since the world began, no ear has heard, and no eye has seen a God like you, who works for those who wait for him!
—Isaiah 64:4 (NLT)

B usy. Busy. Busy. Many of My children are so very busy, they think they just don't have time to spend with Me. So they live and work in their own strength. And when that runs out, they either cry out to Me for help or turn away angrily.

But it's so much better to live close to Me all along—depending on My Strength and trusting Me for help. If you live this way, you will *do* less but actually get more of the important things done.

When you take time for Me, your unhurried way of living will stand out in this rush, rush world. Some people may think you are lazy, but many more will be blessed by your peacefulness.

So make time to wait with Me, and I will *work for you* while you wait.

READ ON YOUR OWN

John 15:5; Psalm 36:9

Your Refuge and Strength

God is our refuge and strength,
always ready to help in times of trouble.
—Psalm 46:1 (NLT)

There is so much bad news in the world. Just watching the evening news can be like seeing a horror movie. There are reports of murders, terrorists, floods, earthquakes, tornadoes. If you focus all on those dangers and forget I am taking care of you, fear will creep into your mind.

Remember: I am your Refuge and Strength, always ready to help in times of trouble. You don't have to be afraid of anything, because I am in control. Every day, I pour out My grace in countless places and situations. I shower blessings on your planet—and even many miracles—but the evening news doesn't report these things.

Don't focus on all the bad news; focus on Me. See My Presence all around you, and remember that I am your Refuge.

READ ON YOUR OWN

Psalm 46:1–3; Psalm 89:15

December 29

Tiny Steps of Trust

*Trust in the L*ORD *forever, for the L*ORD*, the L*ORD*, is the Rock eternal.*
—Isaiah 26:4

Trust Me with every fiber of your being! The more you choose to trust Me, the more I can do in you and through you.

I want you to trust Me in the big things, the crisis moments, the important decisions. I also want you to trust Me in the small things, the everyday moments, the decisions you hardly even think about.

Trusting Me in the everyday things tells Me that your trust is a daily habit—*not* something you forget about until times get tough.

I care just as much about your tiny steps of trust as I do about your gigantic leaps of faith. You may think that no one notices, but the One who is always beside you sees everything—and rejoices!

READ ON YOUR OWN

Psalm 40:4; Psalm 56:3–4; Psalm 62:8; Isaiah 26:3

One of a Kind

*Dear friends, we should love each other, because love comes from
God. The person who loves has become God's child and knows God.*
—1 John 4:7 (ICB)

You are one of a kind. There is no one else like you. That is why I
created a path just for you. As you go with Me down your path,
you become more and more the person I designed you to be.

Because you are one of a kind, the path you are traveling along
is not the same as the paths of others. They are following the
paths that I created just for them.

However, in My own mysterious ways, I have made you able to
follow your own path while also staying in close contact with
others. In fact, the more you stay in step with Me—because you
love Me—the more freely you can love other people.

Be amazed at how wonderfully I work in your life. The more you
follow My path for you, the more you become who you really are.
And the more you love Me, the more you can love others.

READ ON YOUR OWN

2 Corinthians 5:17; Ephesians 2:10; 1 John 4:8; John 15:4

December 31

My Peace

Peace I leave with you; my peace I give you.
—John 14:27

As this year comes to a close, receive My Peace. This is still your deepest need. And I, your Prince of Peace, am waiting to pour Myself into you to meet this need. Your emptiness and My abundance are a perfect match.

I created you as a jar of clay, designed for holy use. Don't try to fill yourself with things from this world. I want you to be filled with My Presence and Peace.

Thank Me for My peaceful Presence, no matter how you are feeling right now. Whisper My Name in tender love. Worship Me in songs of praise. And My Peace, which already lives in your spirit, will work its way through every bit of you—little by little.

READ ON YOUR OWN

Isaiah 9:6; 2 Corinthians 4:7; John 14:26

About the Author

Sarah Young, author of the bestselling 365-day devotionals *Jesus Calling*® and *Jesus Listens*, was committed to helping people connect with Jesus and the Bible. Her books have sold more than 45 million copies worldwide. *Jesus Calling*® has appeared on all major bestseller lists. Sarah's writings include *Jesus Calling*®, *Jesus Listens*, *Jesus Always*, *Jesus Today*®, *Jesus Lives*™, *Dear Jesus*, *Jesus Calling*® *for Little Ones*, *Jesus Calling*® *Bible Storybook*, *Jesus Calling*®: *365 Devotions for Kids*, and more, each encouraging readers in their journeys toward intimacy with Christ. Sarah believed praying for her readers was a privilege and God-given responsibility and did so daily even amidst her own health challenges.

Connect with Jesus Calling at:
Facebook.com/JesusCalling
Instagram.com/JesusCalling
YouTube.com/jesuscallingbook
Pinterest.com/Jesus_Calling